BRIEF INTERVENTION
FOR SCHOOL PROBLEMS

The Guilford School Practitioner Series

EDITORS
STEPHEN N. ELLIOTT, PhD   JOSEPH C. WITT, PhD
Vanderbilt University   Louisiana State University, Baton Rouge

Brief Intervention
for School Problems
Second Edition
OUTCOME-INFORMED STRATEGIES

◆ ◆ ◆

John J. Murphy
Barry L. Duncan

◆

THE GUILFORD PRESS
New York   London

© 2007 The Guilford Press
A Division of Guilford Publications, Inc.
72 Spring Street, New York, NY 10012
www.guilford.com

Printed in the United States of America

This book is printed on acid-free paper.

Last digit is print number: 9 8 7 6 5 4 3 2 1

The authors have checked with sources believed to be reliable in their
efforts to provide information that is complete and generally in accord with
the standards of practice that are accepted at the time of publication.
However, in view of the possibility of human error or changes in medical
sciences, neither the authors, nor the editor and publisher, nor any other
party who has been involved in the preparation or publication of this work
warrants that the information contained herein is in every respect accurate
or complete, and they are not responsible for any errors or omissions or the
results obtained from the use of such information. Readers are encouraged
to confirm the information contained in this book with other sources.

Library of Congress Cataloging-in-Publication Data
Murphy, John J. (John Joseph), 1955–
    Brief intervention for school problems : outcome-informed strategies /
by John J. Murphy and Barry L. Duncan. — 2nd ed.
        p. cm. — (The Guilford school practitioner series)
    Includes bibliographical references and index.
    ISBN-13: 978-1-59385-492-8 (hardcover : alk. paper)
    ISBN-10: 1-59385-492-7 (hardcover : alk. paper)
        1. Problem children—Education—United States—Case
studies.   2. Educational counseling—United States—Case
studies.   3. Student assistance programs—United States—Case
studies.   4. Problem children—Services for—United States—
Case studies.   I. Duncan, Barry L.   II. Title.   III. Series.
LC4802.M87 2007
371.93—dc22
                                                    2007015226

*In honor of John's mother, Mary Murphy,
and in memory of Barry's mother-in-law,
Evelyn Adler*

About the Authors

♦

John J. Murphy, PhD, Professor of Psychology and Counseling at the University of Central Arkansas, is a prominent practitioner, author, and trainer of brief therapy and strengths-based approaches with children, adolescents, and school problems. Dr. Murphy is a former public school teacher who previously was named one of the top five school psychologists in the United States. He continues to practice in schools and to train people throughout the United States and overseas. For more information, see *www.drjohnmurphy.com*.

Barry L. Duncan, PsyD, a therapist and trainer with over 17,000 hours of clinical experience, is Co-Director of the Institute for the Study of Therapeutic Change. Dr. Duncan has received numerous awards for his contributions to the mental health field. He has authored or coauthored over 100 publications, including 14 books, and has discussed his self-help books on *The Oprah Winfrey Show*, *The View*, and other television programs.

Preface

◆

When Chris Jennison of The Guilford Press asked about a second edition, both of us were involved in multiple projects and were reluctant to take on another. But the prospect of working together again and sharing what we find exciting in our field, perhaps even revolutionary new developments in brief intervention, was too compelling to turn down. We hope that our passion for the ideas and the spirit of our friendship infuse the pages of this book.

While the first-edition theme of changing school problems by enlisting the talents of the true heroes of intervention—students, parents, and teachers—remains intact, this edition includes several changes beyond empirical updates. After Chapter 1 introduces the book with a short client example that illustrates the amazing and often humbling resiliencies of the children we serve, Chapter 2 presents the latest research on effective intervention and change. This research solidifies the all-important role of clients in successful outcomes—their strengths and resources, perceptions of the client–practitioner alliance, and ongoing feedback about outcomes. The empirical findings in Chapter 2 are translated into the three practical guidelines: (1) The Client Knows Best, (2) Reliance on the Alliance, and (3) If at First You Don't Succeed, Try Something Different.

Rooted in these guidelines, Chapter 3 introduces two flexible interview-ing formats for approaching school problems and the people who expe-rience them: *solution building* and *problem busting*. Both methods build on the resources and ideas that every client brings to the change process while providing the practitioner with rapid intervention possibilities. Entirely new to this edition, Chapter 4 describes a dramatic shift in the provision of school services: increasing effectiveness via client feedback about the benefit and fit of intervention. The chapter details the nuts and bolts of outcome management, which enables practitioners to enhance the results and accountability of their services. Chapters 5 and 6 pull it all together through two full-length client examples involving elemen-tary and high school students. Also new to this edition, Chapter 7 tack-les the controversial topic of medication for young people with school problems. The skyrocketing rates of drug prescriptions led us to con-clude that *not* addressing this issue would ignore a growing reality impacting children and those who work with them. Finally, the last chapter takes a "to-the-point" attitude toward frequently asked ques-tions about brief intervention as well as the controversial issues of the day.

The second edition retains the pragmatic focus of the original. We provide thorough coverage of the research, but specify the day-to-day implications of the findings. We present a straightforward account of what is known, and put to rest the customary equivocation found in typ-ical writings about research. In short, we strive to translate research into practical guidelines in a way that pays more than the traditional lip ser-vice to the gap between research and practice. We intend to close at least a portion of that gap.

Having spent the bulk of our careers as practitioners, we wanted to "keep it real" by making sure that every concept and technique in the book is applicable to real problems in the real world. If we have not done it, it is not in the book. All of the client examples are real, and many include word-for-word dialogue from intervention sessions with students, parents, and teachers (a list of these examples can be found in Appendix A). Although names and details have been altered for privacy purposes, every client example remains true to what really happened. We are well aware of the many and varied demands of everyday practice in the schools, and remain mindful of these challenges throughout our writing.

To clarify our terminology, *client* refers to anyone with whom the practitioner works to change a school problem—student, teacher, parent, administrator, and so forth. *School practitioner* includes school psychologists, counselors, social workers, therapists, and others who consult on school problems. Finally, *intervention* encompasses counseling, parent–teacher consultation, and any other change-focused activity aimed at resolving the problem.

We are grateful to many people for their support and contributions to our work on this and other projects. We have greatly benefited from our discussions and collaborations with the following colleagues who share our passion for being useful to clients: Jacqueline Sparks, Ioan Rees, Scott Miller, Bruce Wampold, Art Gillaspy, Michael Lambert, and Kelly Wilson, as well as the practitioners of the "Heroic Agencies" list (*www.talkingcure.com*). A special thanks to Jacqueline Sparks, our coauthor on Chapter 7, for her major contributions to the discussion of medication, children, and schools. To the practitioners, trainers, graduate students, and other workshop participants throughout the world, your feedback and comments have been invaluable to our ideas and practices. We appreciate the proofreading and feedback provided by several graduate students and practitioners, including Eva Windsor, Cari Calhoun, Kasey McClain, Beth Waller, Matthew Pickard, Chad Anderson, and Leah Mohlke. We are also indebted to the University of Central Arkansas for grant funding, and to David Skotko, Chair of the Psychology and Counseling Department, for his support of the book. To Chris Jennison and Craig Thomas of The Guilford Press, thank you for your kindness and professionalism, your interest in the second edition, and your patience as we completed it. Most importantly, we owe an incalculable debt to our wives, Debbie and Karen, and our children, Tom, Erin, and Maura Murphy, and Jesse and Matthew Duncan, for their inspiration, encouragement, and patience. When our spouses told us we were well matched in our perseverance and dedication to this project, we had no choice but to take it as a compliment!

Brief Intervention for School Problems integrates the most potent factors of change into a respectful and pragmatic approach to school intervention. Our greatest hope is that it will be of immediate and practical assistance to you and your clients. As you read through the book, know that we are honored by your decision to join us in learning from the greatest teachers of all: the students, parents, teachers, and others who we are privileged to serve.

Contents

◆

CHAPTER 1

♦ ♦ ♦

Kenny

An Introduction to What Works

♦

Until lions have their historians, tales of hunting
will always glorify the hunter.
—AFRICAN PROVERB

Several years ago, a third-grade student named Kenny was referred to
the school practitioner by his teacher for a psychological evaluation. He
received a failing grade in math for the first quarter and barely passed
most of his other subjects. In addition to the assessment of intellectual
ability and academic skills, state regulations required the completion of
a social/family history form. This form was routinely completed as the
first step of the evaluation process.

When asked about his family background during the first few minutes of the meeting, Kenny reported that he witnessed his father's mur-
der when he was 5 years old. At age 6, he was removed from his
mother's custody when she was charged with child abuse. Kenny was
placed with his aunt, who was caring for several children of her own at
the time. One older brother was in jail for burglary, and another was on
parole. It was Kenny's third different school since kindergarten, and his
aunt was preparing to move again. The practitioner had heard similar
stories from other students, but his reaction to this one was different.

1

In the midst of a routine psychological evaluation, the practitioner was stunned by the details of Kenny's family history. Although it was probably only a couple minutes, it felt like hours as Kenny and the practitioner sat there staring at the table in silence—Kenny occasionally sobbing, the practitioner wondering what to say to a third grader who had experienced more chaos in 9 short years than some people do in a lifetime. The practitioner finally broke the silence:

SCHOOL PRACTITIONER (SP): Kenny, with all the stuff that's happened in your life, how do you manage to keep hanging in there, coming to school and trying to do the schoolwork?

KENNY: My aunt always tells me to never give up because quitters don't make it.

SP: Hmm. What else does your aunt say or do that helps you hang in there and keep trying?

KENNY: She's always saying these things about "trying hard" and "doing your best" and "giving your all" and stuff like that.

SP: And it helps you hang in there and keep trying when she says these things?

KENNY: Sometimes.

SP: So she says these things and it helps you.

KENNY: Yeah. And she tells me I'll be the only one in the family to graduate from high school.

SP: Wow. Is that something you want to do?

KENNY: (*Nods head "yes."*) I want to graduate.

SP: Why is it important for you to graduate?

KENNY: If I graduate I can get a good job.

SP: What do you mean?

KENNY: If you graduate you can get a good job. They pay you a lot of money and you can buy your own house.

Kenny became more engaged as the conversation shifted from what was missing or not working to what *was* working in his life. He leaned forward in his chair, his speech became livelier, and he looked at the practitioner instead of staring at the floor. Kenny was now an active participant.

When asked what else made things better, Kenny reported that his older brother Robert occasionally helped him with homework. He added that it took him longer than others to do math, and it helped when his teacher gave him extra time. Building on these resources, the practitioner worked with Kenny, the teacher, and his aunt to amplify what had helped him persevere in school and elsewhere. His teacher gladly provided extra time in math. Robert also stepped up his efforts to help Kenny with homework. Surprised to hear of the positive effect of her homespun sayings, Kenny's aunt was delighted to continue her simple words of wisdom. The teacher incorporated similar words of support. Finally, the practitioner and Kenny collaborated to expand his aunt's sayings into self-talk strategies to cope with tough situations at school and elsewhere.

Kenny provided all of the necessary material for change. Brief intervention strategies emerged from Kenny's resources—his story of resilience—that helped him to survive and persist in school and elsewhere. The practitioner followed Kenny's lead and applied what worked in Kenny's life to the referral problem.

Kenny's heroic story inspired a watershed experience for the practitioner. Before meeting Kenny, the practitioner believed that change was about the intervention, not the individual. Change, he thought, emerged from the practitioner's competence in designing expert interventions and selling them to the client. Practitioners were the heroes of intervention. But Kenny changed all that. His story of courage and resilience, as the epigraph beginning this chapter suggests, overshadowed the hunter's tale of the hunt—the story of diagnosis and deficiencies. Kenny, the practitioner came to realize, was the real lion of change.

Kenny did not qualify for special education services. He continued to struggle academically, but the strategies that arose from his experience served him well. As the school year ended, Kenny made a point to proudly inform the practitioner that he was promoted to the fourth grade.

CONCLUSIONS

Kenny provides a backdrop for the rest of the book. Chapter 2 reviews empirical literature to explain how change occurred with Kenny, and translates 40 years of research into pragmatic guidelines for school-based practice. Subsequent chapters illustrate these guidelines with practical examples of intervention for a wide range of clients and problems. Kenny also proves that change can occur quickly and with limited practitioner time. Effective intervention resulted from a 15-minute conversation sandwiched between the routine chores of evaluation. This book hopes to convince you that every contact, no matter how brief, is an opportunity for change.

CHAPTER 2

♦ ♦ ♦

Empirical Foundations
of Effective Intervention

♦

The great tragedy of science—the slaying
of a beautiful hypothesis by an ugly fact.
—T. H. HUXLEY

Research on intervention effectiveness has either bored or intimidated generations of school practitioners. Those in the trenches see little to entice them in the empirical literature about outcome. But all that is changing. What we now know is that the secret of Kenny's success has been identified, quantified, and described. This chapter demystifies the research, examines the most potent elements of change, and reveals the contribution of technique to be small relative to other more powerful ingredients. In spite of the overwhelming empirical support for these factors, practical implications remain obscure. Chapter 2 translates the research into three pragmatic guidelines for school-based practice. Finally, this chapter stresses the value of forming alliances with students, parents, and teachers, and outlines practical steps for doing so.

5

WHY INTERVENTION REALLY WORKS

Research has led to an inarguable conclusion that is good news for both school professionals and clients alike: Intervention is effective in resolving human problems. The good news of intervention usefulness, however, has been accompanied by a rabbitlike propagation of different models. Over the years, new models of helping arrived with the regularity of the Book of the Month Club's main selection. Most professed to have captured the true essence of psychological dysfunction as well as the best remedies.

In the hope of proving their pet approaches superior, a generation of investigators ushered in the age of comparative clinical trials. Winners and losers were to be determined. Thus, behavioral, psychoanalytic, client-centered, cognitive, and other models were pitted against each other in a battle of the brands. Nonetheless, all this sound and fury produced an unexpected bonfire of the vanities (Hubble, Duncan, & Miller, 1999). Put another way, reiterating Huxley's epigraph introducing this chapter, science slew a beautiful hypothesis with an ugly fact. The underlying premise of the comparative studies, that one intervention approach would prove superior to others, received virtually no support. Besides the occasional finding for a particular model, the critical mass of data revealed no differences in effectiveness between the various treatments. Despite the Herculean efforts of legions of model worshippers, no one succeeded in declaring any religion to be the best.

These findings have been creatively summarized by quoting the dodo bird from *Alice's Adventures in Wonderland*, who said, "Everybody has won and all must have prizes" (Carroll, 1865/1962). It was Saul Rosenzweig (1936) who first invoked the dodo's words to illustrate his prophetic observation of the equivalent success of diverse intervention models (Duncan, 2002). Almost 40 years later, Luborsky, Singer, and Luborsky (1975) empirically validated Rozenzweig's conclusion in their now-classic review of comparative clinical trials. They dubbed their findings of no differences among models the "dodo bird verdict." The dodo bird verdict has become one of the most replicated findings in the psychological literature across a broad array of research designs, problems, populations, and settings (Asay & Lambert, 1999), including marriage and family approaches (Shadish & Baldwin, 2002) and child and adolescent therapies (Dennis et al., 2004; Spielmans, 2006).

Consider a recent replication, particularly germane for school practitioners, the Cannabis Youth Treatment (CYT) study (Dennis et al., 2004). This state-of-the-art study randomly assigned 600 youth with multiple problems (including marijuana addiction) to three different intervention models (cognitive-behavioral therapy, motivational interviewing, and multidimensional family therapy) at two different "doses" (5 and 12 weeks; all included long-term follow-up and support). Overall, the different types *and* doses of intervention worked with about the same effectiveness! Despite the claims of snake-oil peddlers and model maniacs, no winner has emerged for cannabis addiction or any other problem plaguing youth in today's schools.

Meta-analytic studies, which allow researchers to comb through the vast literature and draw conclusions from huge collections of data, lend even further credence to the dodo bird verdict. In researcher Bruce Wampold's comprehensive 1997 review of the outcome literature, some 277 studies conducted from 1970 to 1995 were analyzed to determine which models have yielded the most robust results (Wampold et al., 1997). This comprehensive review once again verified that no approach has reliably demonstrated superiority over any other. This also holds true in a recent meta-analytic study of child and adolescent approaches (Miller, Wampold, & Varhely, in press).

The fact that the dodo bird verdict has emerged by *accident*—while researchers were trying to prove the superiority of their own models— makes it even more compelling. It is a finding free of researcher bias. But what does it mean? As Rosenzweig amazingly said some 71 years ago, because all approaches appear equal in effectiveness, there must be common factors that overshadow any perceived or presumed differences among approaches. Intervention works, but our understanding of how it works cannot be found in the insular explanations of the different theoretical orientations.

Figure 2.1 depicts the four common factors of change and their percentage contribution to a positive outcome *regardless of the theoretical orientation or professional discipline of the helper* (Asay & Lambert, 1999): (1) client factors (40%), (2) relationship factors (30%), (3) placebo factors (15%), and (4) model factors (15%). The research summarized in Figure 2.1 is extensive, is decades old, and represents a broad range of problems, clients, practitioners, and settings.

Since the publication of the first edition of this book, Bruce Wampold (2001) published a meta-analytic review of the outcome

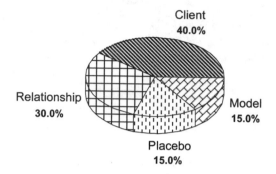

FIGURE 2.1. Common factors of change and their percentage contribution to successful outcomes. Data from Asay and Lambert (1999).

research. It has not only bolstered our perspective of the common factors, it has significantly broadened our appreciation of the potency of client and relationship factors.

THE INTERVENTION PIE

Imagine that change, or what makes intervention effective, is your favorite pie. Corresponding to the four factors listed earlier, your pie has four essential ingredients.

The Filling: Client Factors

Clients, perhaps especially students, have long been portrayed by the Killer D's (diagnosis, disorder, dysfunction, disease, disability, deficit, damaged, delinquent, etc.). Rarely are students, parents, and teachers cast in the role of the chief agent of change or even mentioned in connection with the newest line of fashionable intervention techniques. Tallman and Bohart's (1999) review of the research makes clear, however, that the client is the single most potent contributor to outcome, through the client's internal and external resources. These factors might include persistence, openness, faith, optimism, a supportive grandmother, or membership in a religious community, all operative in a client's life before he or she encounters a school practitioner. They also include serendipitous interactions between such inner strengths and happenstance, such as a new school or a crisis successfully negotiated. Asay and Lambert (1999) ascribe 40% of improvement during intervention to client factors. Wampold's (2001) meta-analysis attributes an amazing 87% to these so-called extratherapeutic factors. *This perspective about change suggests a radical revamping of our ideas about clients and about what intervention should look like.*

Students, parents, and teachers, therefore, are the filling in our intervention pie. The main ingredient to any pie is the filling, whether it is chocolate, lemon, custard, or rhubarb. The filling represents change that is attributed to client factors because, whether at 40% or 87%, client factors represent the largest contribution to the change process. Intervening without a dependence on the client's resources is like eating a pie without filling. Kenny is a prime example of client factors at work. *Effective intervention encourages student, teacher, and parent resources to take center stage because they are the most potent factors available.*

Chance or fortuitous events also contribute to problem resolution—seemingly spontaneous changes initiated by clients during the course of intervention. These changes are common and highlight the capability of clients to apply their resources to solve problems. For example, an early study looking at when change occurs found that the majority of change in successful intervention happens earlier rather than later; about 65% of clients changed in the first eight sessions (Howard, Kopta, Krause, & Orlinsky, 1986). Because the practitioners in this study were primarily psychodynamic, it is remarkable that clients achieved the lion's share of change far before the model would predict—arguably before the "real" treatment even began! Similarly, Hansen and Lambert (2003) report that up to 35% of clients are so-called early responders (in the first three meetings), changing before active intervention begins. These findings suggest that change itself is a potent client factor, highlighting the inherent capacity of clients to overcome life's impasses.

Consider Charles, a first grader referred by his mother and teacher to improve classroom behavior. The problems involved a classmate named Dwayne. Intervention focused on helping Charles to "resist the temptation" to respond to Dwayne's teasing. Some positive changes occurred, but paled in comparison to the changes that followed a chance event. Charles and Dwayne saw each other in the neighborhood and decided to ride bikes together. They did the same thing the next day.

Within a week, they considered themselves good friends. Charles' classroom behavior improved after their serendipitous encounter. *Effective intervention capitalizes on chance and other naturally occurring changes in the client's life.*

The Crust: Relationship Factors

Next to what the client brings, the client's perception of the relationship is responsible for most of the gains resulting from intervention. Relationship factors, or what is now referred to as the "alliance," account for 30% of successful outcome (Asay & Lambert, 1999). The alliance emphasizes collaboration, a partnership between the client and practitioner to achieve the client's goals (Bordin, 1979). Research repeatedly finds that a positive alliance is one of the best predictors of outcome (Martin, Garske, & Davis, 2000).

Consider findings specifically related to youth intervention: Child–practitioner and parent–practitioner alliances are both related to positive changes in the child; parent–practitioner alliance is related to improvement in parenting skills and interactions at home; and child and parent evaluations of the alliance are more predictive than helper evaluations (Kazdin, Marciano, & Whitley, 2005; Shirk & Karver, 2003). Finally, in the CYT study, the alliance predicted outcome as well as both dropouts and postintervention cannabis use (Shelef, Diamond, Diamond, & Liddle, 2005). *It is critical for school practitioners to attend closely to the alliance and regularly monitor its quality.*

If you are not convinced that the alliance should be central to your ideas about change, consider the Wampold (2001) meta-analytic perspective of the alliance. He portions 54% of the variance attributed to the impact of intervention to the alliance. Putting this into perspective, the amount of change attributable to the alliance is about seven times that which is attributable to the specific model or technique.

Returning to our pie metaphor, the alliance comprises the crust or container for the filling. The crust allows the filling to have the structure and space to be appreciated. The relationship contains clients comfortably while allowing their resources to take center stage.

Research on the power of the alliance reflects over 1,000 findings and counting (Orlinsky, Rønnestad, & Willutzki, 2004). We must set aside the intellectual appeal of theoretical models, the promises of flashy techniques, the charisma of masters, and the marketing acumen of snake-oil peddlers. *The research indicates that intervention works if students, parents, and teachers experience the relationship positively and are active participants.* Later in this chapter we translate these findings into practical ways to build strong alliances and invite client participation. Monitoring the alliance figures prominently in becoming outcome informed (Chapter 4).

The Pie in the Sky: Placebo Factors

Following client and relationship factors in impact are placebo/expectancy factors—the portion of improvement deriving from clients' knowledge of being helped, the instillation of hope, and the credibility of intervention. Also included here is the allegiance of the practitioner to his or her chosen methods or techniques. Placebo/expectancy accounts for 15% of successful outcome (Asay & Lambert, 1999).

To continue our pie metaphor, imagine that you are visiting your mother. You especially enjoy her version of your favorite pie. After fantasizing about the pie all week, you walk through the door of Mom's house and a wave of aroma envelops you. You quickly walk into the kitchen and there it is, in all its glory. The pie's mouthwatering visual presentation, enticing aroma, and arousal of your hopes for culinary delight illustrate placebo/expectancy.

Starting any change endeavor tantalizes clients with visions of a delicious future and offers a healthy helping of hope to a distasteful present. Research shows that merely expecting help goes a long way in counteracting demoralization, mobilizing hope, and advancing improvement (Frank & Frank, 1991). Hope and expectancy also give people a measurable advantage in many areas of life—in academic achievement, managing major illness, and dealing with difficult job situations (Goleman, 1991).

Teachers and parents often enlist our help when everything seems to be falling apart. They feel defeated and demoralized. The creation of hope is greatly influenced by the practitioner's attitude as well as the credibility of the intervention. Pessimistic attitudes are likely to minimize the effects of placebo factors. Practitioners' belief that change will occur as well as their confidence in chosen methods instills hope and an expectation for improvement. Creating this atmosphere is not the same as adopting a Pollyannaish, "every cloud has a silver lining" attitude. Rather, hopefulness results from acknowledging both the problem *and* the possibilities. From the client's perspective, the credibility of the intervention is strengthened when it resonates with the client's ideas, experiences, and preferences. *Effective intervention is credible to the client and instills hope when practitioners have faith in the intervention process and client capacities for change.*

Meringue: Model Factors

Models and techniques make up the last of the four factors and contribute 15% to change (Asay & Lambert, 1999). Model/technique factors are the beliefs and procedures unique to specific treatments—the miracle question in solution-focused therapy, desensitization in behavior therapy, and thought stopping in cognitive therapy, as well as the respective theoretical premises attending these practices. Wampold's (2001) meta-analysis assigns an even smaller contribution: Only 1% is attributed to model and technique!

How exactly should models be viewed when so much of change is controlled by other factors? Models provide a structure and focus for conducting intervention, and, more importantly, alternative ways of addressing client concerns when progress is stalling. Models are most helpful when they provide practitioners with novel ways of looking at old situations—when they empower practitioners to *change* rather than *make up their minds about* clients (Miller, Duncan, & Hubble, 1997). With over 400 intervention models to choose from, there is little reason for continued allegiance to a particular approach when it is not producing results. Practitioners and clients can simply go back to the smorgasbord and make another selection.

Returning to the pie metaphor, model factors are represented by the pie's meringue. The meringue enhances the appearance of the pie and embellishes the taste, but it cannot stand well on its own. Without the rest of the pie to give it form and substance, the meringue is nothing but fluff. A model provides the means to an end and focuses our combined efforts but is meaningless without the benefit of client resources, ideas, and active participation. The model is certainly nothing but fluff if it doesn't deliver results, if it does not help students, parents, and teachers reach their goals. As Chapter 4 illustrates, viewing models in this way is key to an outcome-informed approach.

This is not to say that models and techniques are unimportant. *Models that capitalize on client resources, accept client's goals, and establish a better match with client ideas about change are likely to be the most beneficial.*

THREE GUIDELINES FOR EFFECTIVE INTERVENTION

The common factors provide the empirical backdrop for brief, outcome-informed practice. This approach contains no fixed techniques, no invariant patterns in intervention process, and no causal theory regarding the concerns that bring people to see school practitioners. Any interaction with a student, parent, or teacher can be both brief and outcome-informed. This comes about when the practitioner follows three general guidelines that enhance the factors across theories that account for successful outcome: (1) *"The Client Knows Best"* (Chapter 3); (2) *"Reliance on the Alliance"* (Chapter 2); and (3) *"If at First You Don't Succeed, Try Something Different"* (Chapter 4).

Guideline 1. The Client Knows Best: Everything I Needed to Know about Intervention I Learned from a 10-Year-Old

Client factors are, by far, the most powerful contribution to change. These variables are incidental to the intervention model and idiosyncratic to the specific client. Among the client variables frequently mentioned for youth are age/developmental status, youth/parent interpersonal functioning, parental mental health, parental intelligence, family environment, and youth/parent expectancies of efficacy (Karver, Handelsman, Fields, & Bickman, 2005). In the absence of compelling evidence that any of these specific client variables predict outcome, this most potent source of change remains largely uncharted. This situation suggests that specific client qualities cannot be generalized because these factors differ with each client. These unpredictable differences can only emerge one client at a time, one alliance at a time, one practitioner at a time, and one intervention at a time. Chapter 3 illustrates how practitioners can harvest and channel these delightfully unpredictable characteristics of clients toward change.

To illustrate our data-based guideline "The Client Knows Best," consider 10-year-old Molly. Molly was referred by her mother, Janice. Her parents were divorced. She was sleeping in Janice's bed and having trouble adjusting to a new apartment, school, and friends. After an intake interview, Molly was labeled as coming from a "dysfunctional family." Bestowed the diagnosis of "separation-anxiety disorder," she was referred to a weekly children's social skills group.

After a few weeks in group, Janice reported that Molly was experiencing nightmares. The group counselor responded by seeing Molly individually. The following goals were established: (1) increase Molly's understanding of being in control of her behavior, (2) relieve her fears about moving and adjusting to a new school, (3) raise her self-esteem, and (4) help her return to her room to sleep.

After 6 months of concurrent group and individual intervention, there was little improvement. Janice then requested a female counselor. Because Molly asked if her counselor ever felt ugly, it was surmised that Molly had low self-esteem. The new, individual intervention now revolved around playing a game "to see what themes came out." The counselor also wondered whether Molly was a victim of sexual abuse. Her goals for Molly were to (1) explore for sexual abuse and (2) investigate Molly's feelings about her father.

Still concerned about her daughter's lack of progress, Janice requested a psychiatric evaluation. The evaluation noted that Molly still slept in her mother's room and that somatic complaints remained. An antidepressant was prescribed to relieve Molly's separation anxiety. Molly, in twice-weekly treatment for over a year and now on medication, was fast becoming a candidate for placement in a school program for emotionally disturbed students. Dedicated to her daughter's welfare and dissatisfied with the care, Janice discontinued the medication and sought different help.

In both the group and individual interventions, the counselors neglected to ask Molly for her ideas about her predicament or enlist her resources to solve her dilemma. Molly was assessed, her problems were categorized, and the interventions were prescribed. What she brought to the table—her resources and ideas—were immaterial. The explanatory labels (dysfunctional family, separation-anxiety disorder) said it all.

In the first meeting with the new practitioner, Molly was asked what she believed would be helpful for resolving the problem. Molly expressed astonishment that someone finally wanted her opinion. She then suggested that she could barricade herself in her bed with pillows and stuffed animals to "ward off" her nightmares and fears. In the second contact she reported that her plan was working.

The following excerpts come from the third meeting. They reflect Molly's observations about what was helpful, and not helpful, in her experiences with counselors. Molly makes it clear that her previous counselors attempted to bake a pie without the most essential ingredient.

SCHOOL PRACTITIONER (SP): Well, how is it going?

MOLLY: Just fine. I'm sleeping in my own room. I've been in my own room since I've told you about it.

SP: That's great! That's wonderful! I'm impressed by that still.

MOLLY: Counselors just don't understand . . . you [the client] also have the solutions, for yourself, but they say, "Let's try this and let's try that" and they're not helping. So, what I'm saying to all psychiatrists is we have the answers, *we just need someone to help us bring them to the front of our head. It's like they're locked in an attic or something.*

Commentary: In her own quaint, 10-year-old fashion, Molly explains how the expert model of her previous helpers missed the mark. Simply put, the models were unnecessary for her improvement and actually prolonged her stay in counseling. She maintains that it is better to ask clients for their opinions about their problems and solutions. Molly now speaks about what it was like for her to find her own solution.

MOLLY: I feel a lot better now that I came up with the solution to sleep in my own room, and I did it and I'm proud of myself. And, I couldn't be proud of myself if you told me, "How about if you barricade yourself in with pillows? Maybe that'll work." And if it works you are not going to get all the credit and you are going to want credit for doing it and everything but because the psychiatrist told you to do it you are not going to get as much. And I'm not being greedy or anything but you want to do it yourself.

SP: That's right.

MOLLY: And you want to be proud of what you've done.

SP: Exactly.

MOLLY: So basically what I am saying is (*pause*) *you don't get as much joy out of doing something when someone else thought of it.*

Commentary: Molly derived her own solution and it enhanced her self-esteem. When provided the opportunity, Molly revealed her inventiveness. When given the space, her resources became apparent. Her "pillow brigade" worked and she continued to sleep in her room without nightmares. Her other complaints also resolved in short order.

As soon as Molly's resources and ideas were allowed central consideration, when she was regarded as a competent partner by inviting her solutions, her sleep disturbance ended. We present her situation not to condemn the previous helpers, suggest we hold magical solutions, or imply that all clients will be similar. Instead, we see her story as a good example of "The Client Knows Best" guideline.

Guideline 2. Reliance on the Alliance

We hope we have made a strong case for the importance of the alliance in any change endeavor, and that whether dealing with students, parents, or teachers, it is their perceptions of the alliance that are predictive of success, not the practitioners. The alliance is our most powerful ally in intervention success and represents the most influence that practitioners can have over outcome. Do not underestimate its power. Recall the Cannabis Youth Treatment study: The alliance not only predicted outcome and dropouts, it predicted cannabis use at 3- and 6-month follow-ups. The power of the alliance is enduring.

Given our dependence on the alliance, we will unfold it here in detail as a foundation (the crust) for the rest of this book and the intervention process. The alliance data suggest that intervention works if clients experience the relationship positively, perceive it to be relevant to their concerns and goals, and are active participants. Bordin (1979) classically defines the alliance as comprising three interacting elements: (1) a relationship bond between the practitioner and client, (2) agreement on the goals of intervention, and (3) agreement on the tasks of intervention.

Connecting to Students, Parents, and Teachers: The Relational Bond

School practitioner attitude is critical to developing a relational bond. Part and parcel of this attitude is the belief that the alliance is the master to be served. To implement this attitude, we have found it useful to think of each meeting as a first date (without the romantic overtones), in which we consciously put our best foot forward, actively woo the client's favor, and entice his or her participation. Since the relationship is formed early, close attention should be paid to the client's initial perceptions and reactions. Because clients vary widely in their experience of what constitutes a good relationship, practitioner flexibility is important. Conveying to clients that their perspectives, including dissatisfactions, are valued and will be acted upon sends a powerful message.

We pay particular attention to what excites clients: When do they lean forward, raise their voice, have sparkle in their eyes? What topics and ways of relating raise their activity and engagement? Practitioners also need to be alert to cues that signal problems because clients are often reluctant to communicate negative feelings and their dissatisfaction (Hill, Nutt-Williams, Heaton, Thompson, & Rhodes, 1996). Chapter 4 provides a systematic method of detecting alliance problems.

In addition to continual monitoring and flexibility, a useful way of thinking about practitioner relational responses is the idea of *validation*— a process in which the client's struggle is respected, perhaps representing a critical juncture in the client's life. Validation reflects a genuine acceptance of the client at face value and includes an empathic search for justification of the client's experience in the context of trying circumstances (Duncan, Solovey, & Rusk, 1992). Parents and teachers are often wary about practitioner judgments. Validation helps them breathe a sigh of relief and know that blame is not a part of our game: We are on their team. Questions to consider:

- What are the invalidations contained in the client's story? How is the client's experience being discounted or contradicted by the client or others? How is the client being blamed for his or her difficulties?
- What other circumstances have contributed to this situation? How can I place the client's situation in a context that explains and justifies his or her behavior or feelings? How can I give the client credit for trying to do the right thing?
- How is this experience representative of an important crossroad in the client's life or a statement about his or her identity?
- Put the client's experience in the following format: No wonder

you feel or behave this way (*fill in with client circumstance*), given that (*fill in the ways you have discovered to justify his or her responses*).

- Now that the client is validated, what different conclusions are reached? Did any other courses of action emerge?

Consider Margaret, a sixth-grade teacher who asked for a consult regarding Robert, a student who was really getting under her skin. Margaret, a veteran teacher known for her ability to handle tough kids and therefore certain to be "rewarded" with several in her class each year, had not requested a consult previously. She was visibly nervous and perhaps embarrassed when she first spoke to the practitioner. Margaret shared information about Robert's classroom problems. She also intimated that she had "lost it" with Robert and his parents, and perhaps was "not able to cut it anymore." She reported how she had caught him going through her desk and yelled at him—not her usual response—and then got into an argument with his parents when they didn't acknowledge the seriousness of Robert's behavior. The practitioner patiently listened and encouraged Margaret to unfold her story until she was satisfied that the practitioner understood her dilemma. Margaret was tentative in her presentation and often looked like she expected to be criticized. The practitioner responded with validating comments.

> "Although you didn't respond to this student the way you would have liked, no wonder you lost it with him and his parents. He has been a thorn in your side all year and you have patiently put a lot of effort and time into helping him with both his behavior and his academics, not to mention all the discussions with his parents even though, from all appearances, they have done little at home to support your efforts. And all this on top of a large class with too many tough kids—no wonder you are frustrated, and this kid has stretched your usual high standards . . ."

The practitioner replaced the self-invalidations ("lost it" and "not able to cut it anymore") with validating comments. Margaret sighed and relaxed, knowing that the practitioner was in her corner, and collaborated with the practitioner to develop a plan to address the student and his parents.

In summary, serving the alliance master occurs by:

- Being likable, friendly, and responsive (like on a first date).
- Carefully monitoring the client's reaction to comments, explanations, interpretations, questions, and suggestions.
- Being flexible: doing whatever it takes to engage the client. You are many things to many people (friend, partner, parent, child, sibling). Use *your* complexity to fit clients.
- Validating the client: legitimizing the client's concerns and highlight the importance of the client's struggle.

Accepting the Client's Goals

The second aspect of the alliance is the agreement on the goals of intervention. When we talk to clients, we spend little time developing diagnoses or theorizing about possible etiology of the presenting complaint. Rather, the process is comprised of careful listening and alliance monitoring combined with questions aimed at defining and redefining the client's goals.

When we ask clients what they want to be different, we give credibility to their beliefs and values regarding the problem and its solution. We are saying to them that their opinion is important and we are there to serve them. As simple an act as it is, it invites clients to see themselves as collaborators in making their lives better (Murphy, 1999).

Once again, attitude is paramount to the process of eliciting and respecting the client's goals. We accept the client's goals at face value regardless of how they sound because those desires will excite and motivate the client. If we are serving the alliance master, we know that agreement with the client about goals is essential to positive outcome. It begins the process of change, wherever the client may ultimately travel.

Sometimes the goals of students, parents, or teachers do not fit our own sensibilities about what is needed. This may be particularly true if clients carry certain diagnoses or problem scenarios. Consider 14-year-old Sarah, who lived in a group home and was placed in a class for emotionally disordered adolescents. Sarah saw the school practitioner because her teacher considered her to be socially withdrawn. Everyone was worried about Sarah's health because she spent much of her time watching TV and eating snack foods.

But what did Sarah want? Sarah repeatedly expressed her desire to be a Cincinnati Bengals cheerleader, but the school practitioner just couldn't accept this goal. After all, Sarah was not on the school cheerleading squad and was not exactly fit. So no one listened, or even knew why Sarah had such an interesting goal. And the work with Sarah floundered. She rarely spoke and minimally answered questions. The practitioner wanted Sarah to get away from the T.V. and out into the world. He brought his concerns to his colleagues, and they recommended two things: First, that he find out where the desire to be a cheerleader came from, and then find a way to harness Sarah's energy and motivation for that goal.

When the practitioner asked Sarah about her goal, she told the story of growing up watching the Bengals with her dad, who delighted in Sarah's learning and practicing the cheers. Sarah sparkled when she talked of her father, who passed away several years previously; the practitioner noted that it was the most he had ever heard her speak. The practitioner took this experience to heart and often asked Sarah about her father. He also decided to slow down efforts to get Sarah to socialize or exercise (his goals), and instead leaned more toward Sarah's interest in cheerleading. Sarah regularly watched cheerleading contests on ESPN and enjoyed sharing her expertise. These vibrant conversations came to dominate the interactions between Sarah and her counselor.

After a while, Sarah decided to organize a cheerleading squad for the faculty basketball team that played local civic groups for charity. Sarah's involvement with the team ultimately addressed the referral concerns about her social withdrawal and lack of activity. Walking the path cut by student, parent, and teacher goals often reveals alternative routes that would never have been discovered otherwise.

It is sometimes helpful to encourage the student, parent, and teacher to think small (Fisch, Weakland, & Segal, 1982). A change in one aspect of a problem often leads to changes in other areas as well. The wonderful thing about thinking small is that the most easily attainable signal of change becomes symbolic of resolving the entire problem; it creates a momentum and energy like the first domino falling in the seemingly never-ending line of the problem. The first change creates a small chink in the armor of the problem that inspires hope that more change is on the way. Consider these questions related to goal formulation:

- What will you see as the first small sign that things are getting better? If something is already happening, what will be the next sign?
- What will be an indication that things are beginning to turn toward problem improvement?
- What will you be doing differently when this issue is less of a problem?
- If you went to sleep tonight and a miracle occurred and ended this problem, what would be the first thing you would notice at home and school that would be different?
- How will you know that your son doesn't need counseling any more?
- How will things be different in school when you begin paying closer attention during class, or getting to school on time, or turning in more math homework?
- How will you know when he or she is more responsible, has a better attitude, higher self-esteem, and so forth?
- What do you think your teacher will begin to notice about you when things start improving?
- What would convince [your teacher, parents, court-case worker, other referral source(s)] that you need to come here less often or not at all?

Consider Mildred, a charming grandmother who was exasperated with her 10-year-old grandson's school and home problems. Jimmy was diagnosed with attention-deficit/hyperactivity disorder (ADHD) and was already taking medication. When asked what would be different when things were better, Mildred replied that Jimmy would do what he was told. When the practitioner encouraged Mildred to describe the first step toward that goal, she said that she would notice that Jimmy finished his cereal in the morning. Therefore, intervention addressed the morning routine, and Jimmy finished his cereal *and* ultimately started doing his homework. You could read a lot of information about ADHD and likely never find "finishing cereal" as a viable intervention. However, a small but significant success in the morning routine signified that more positive things were on the way: It was the first domino falling that inspired continued improvements. Do not underestimate the power of thinking small. The first glimmer of light can turn into a neon sign shining the way to the ultimate destination.

Tailoring the Tasks of Intervention

The final aspect of the alliance is the agreement on the tasks of intervention. Tasks include specific techniques or points of view, topics of conversation, interview procedures, frequency of meeting, and so on. Another demonstration of our respect for our client's capabilities and our conscious efforts to enlist participation occurs when we ask our clients to help set the tasks of intervention.

In a well-functioning alliance, practitioners and clients jointly work to construct interventions in accordance with clients' preferred outcomes. Traditionally, the search has been for interventions that promote change by validating the practitioner's favored theory. Serving the alliance master requires searching for ideas that promote change by validating the client's view of what is helpful—or what we call the client's theory of change.

THE CLIENT'S THEORY OF CHANGE

An evolving story casts the client as not only the star of the intervention stage, but also the director of the change process (Duncan et al., 1992). We now consider our clients' worldview, their map of the territory, as the determining "theory" for intervention (Duncan, Hubble, & Miller, 1997), directing both the destination desired and the routes of restoration. Rather than reformulating the client's complaint into a favored orientation, practitioners should elevate the student, parent, and teacher's perceptions above theory, and allow the client's view of change to direct intervention choices. Such a process all but guarantees the security of a strong alliance.

LEARNING AND HONORING THE CLIENT'S THEORY

The client has a unique theory waiting for discovery, a framework for change to be used for a successful outcome. We can best explore the client's theory by viewing ourselves as aliens from another planet. We seek a pristine understanding of a close encounter with the client's unique interpretations and cultural experiences. To learn clients' theories, we must adopt their views on their terms, with a very strong bias in their favor.

We begin by listening closely to the client's language. We often take notes so that the exact words that clients choose to describe problems,

desires, and solutions can be recorded. Taking notes, when done unob-
trusively, conveys practitioner interest in, as well as the importance of,
the client's input. We show clients our notes or make copies if they
desire. We explain that the purpose of the notes is to record verbatim
what they say so that we don't miss their descriptions of their experiences and what they want from us. Using clients' language privileges
their understandings and is one more way to keep clients center stage.

What the client wants and how those goals can be accomplished
may be the most important pieces of information that can be obtained.
We believe that clients not only have all that is necessary to resolve problems, but also may have a very good idea about how to do it. Questions
that elicit the client's hunches and educated guesses encourage participation, emphasize the client's input, and provide direct access to the client's theory of change.

- What ideas do you have about what needs to happen for
  improvement to occur?
- Many times people have a pretty good hunch not only about
  what is causing a problem, but also about what will resolve it. Do
  you have a theory of how change is going to happen here?
- Everyone has changed something. How does change usually happen in your life?
- What do you and others do to get it started and keep it going?

In addition, discussion of prior solutions provides an excellent
way for learning the client's theory of change. Exploring solution
attempts enables the practitioner to hear the client's candid evaluation
of previous attempts and their fit with what the client believes to be
helpful.

- What have you tried to help the problem/situation so far? Did it
  help? How did it help? Why didn't it help?
- What have you thought about trying?

Finally, finding out what your role is in the change process is inte-
gral to implementing the client's theory. Some clients want a sounding
board, some want a confidant, some want to brainstorm and problem
solve, and some want an expert to tell them what to do. Explore the client's preferences about your role by asking:

- How do you see me fitting into what you would like to see happen?
- How can I be of most help to you now?
- What role do you see me playing in your endeavor to change this situation?
- Let me make sure I am getting this right. Are you looking for suggestions from me about that situation?
- In what ways do you see me and this process as helpful to attaining your goals?

Honoring the client's theory occurs when a given intervention procedure fits or complements the client's beliefs. We listen and then amplify the stories, experiences, and interpretations the client offers about his or her problems, as well as the client's ideas about how those problems might be addressed. As the client's theory evolves, we implement the client's identified solutions or seek an approach that both fits the client's theory and provides possibilities for change.

Given the frequent hyping of the method-of-the-month, there's a temptation to turn an idea like the client's theory of change into one more invariant prescription. Ask what they'd like to do (or prescribe a ritual, finger waving, etc.), and watch the miracles roll out the office door! This is not what we're saying. All clients will not be like Molly; all solutions will not blossom from the first question about the client's theory. We are also not saying that we never offer ideas or suggestions. Our input is determined one client at a time and is driven by the client's expectations of our role.

Out of the Mouth of Babes: Molly Speaks about the Alliance

Consider Molly's next statements in light of the alliance. Once asked about her convictions, it is as though a long-closed gate has opened.

MOLLY: All my other counselors haven't asked me what I wanted to work on. They asked me questions about the subjects and I am like, I don't really want to answer these questions because, shouldn't I be telling you what I think about this?

SP: (*Laughs.*)

MOLLY: I mean, you are not here to tell me my life or anything. (*Molly and the practitioner laugh.*) I should come in and tell the person, you know, like, "Well, this is happening with this situation and this is happening with this situation."

SP: Um-hm.

MOLLY: But if they are saying, well, your mom tells me that your dad is doing such and such a thing or your grandfather is doing such and such a thing and then there is more stuff . . . it's like, since when did I start having problems with that?

SP: (*Laughs.*)

MOLLY: And when the counselor is telling you what she thinks has happened or what he thinks has happened and it's not really helping because you are just sitting here (*demonstrates her posture, looking down and sounding bored*) going um-hm, um-hm . . . that is why I dreaded going to counseling. It never worked, it never helped because she sat down and started talking—and every now and then I got a sentence in—and she talked the whole hour.

SP: And that wasn't very helpful. It certainly wasn't helpful to your concerns or being able to sleep in your own room.

MOLLY: No way! She ignored me being in Mom's room. So I mean, like, this is probably the most remarkable thing that has ever happened to me. I have come in here and have had somebody actually ask me what I want to do, what I think about the subjects and different things like that, and it helps.

Molly makes it clear she felt discounted and ignored. What she perceived as important was not solicited. Her goals were not given priority, and her collaboration not encouraged. Based on her apparent lack of connection with the practitioner and of agreement regarding goals and tasks, the alliance literature would accurately predict her negative outcome.

Recall that this is the same child placed in a social skills group, diagnosed with separation anxiety disorder, treated with medication, and seen individually for over a year! We say this not to criticize her previous counselors, but rather to emphasize how our chosen models can often blind us to the client's inherent resources. If a gem like Molly can be missed, we must take special caution to ensure we build strong alliances and be mindful of clients' existing abilities.

Returning to Molly one final time, she explains how *not* securing her input, her theory of change, missed the mark.

SP: I knew you'd seen other practitioners about not being able to sleep in your room, but yet . . .

MOLLY: It didn't help. Well, like, my other counselor said, "Let's try this for 5 minutes, then go for 10 minutes, then 15, then go for the whole night." I did it once and I decided, "This isn't helping!" I didn't want to do that thing, so I basically ignored it. . . . They weren't my ideas and they didn't seem right. And counselors are basically telling you what they want you to do. . . . And it is like that they think they are some almighty power or something. (*Both laugh.*)

SP: That drives me nuts when they think they are the almighty word about things.

MOLLY: Like they are God. (*Looks up, extends arms, and sings as though in a choir.*)

SP: (*Both laugh for a while.*) Oh, that is music to my ears, Molly. You know, we think a lot alike.

MOLLY: It's like hang on, I am also somebody. And you laugh at what I mean to be funny, and back at my old counselor, whenever I said something, when I tried to say something about a subject, she just busted up. It's like, hey, I have an opinion too!

SP: She did not take you seriously. . . .

MOLLY: No! And she even said, "I love working with kids and I work really well with kids." (*Leans forward and looks very serious.*) Every kid that she sees, goes for like years. . . .

Commentary: When Molly tried to comply, the process stalled. The ideas were not her own. She resented being told what to do by the almighty counselors. It certainly did not motivate her to do something for herself. And not unlike others, Molly wanted the practitioner to laugh when Molly was trying to be funny—and not when she wasn't. Good advice for a first date, and for a practitioner trying to form a strong alliance. Molly exemplifies "The Client Knows Best" and "Reliance on the Alliance."

Guideline 3. If at First You Don't Succeed, Try Something Different

The relative insignificance of model factors highlights the fact that no one theory has the corner on intervention effectiveness. This is not to suggest that theory is useless. Rather, theories provide helpful lenses to be used depending upon their fit with the client's "frame" and prescription. They are only useful to the extent that they lead to benefit from the client's perspective. Therefore, we must allow the results of our interventions to inform our work. When faced with evidence that clients are not benefiting, we must "try something different."

Try Something Different: The Lessons of the Mental Research Institute

Our third guideline was first suggested by the innovative researchers and clinicians at the Mental Research Institute (MRI) (Fisch et al., 1982; Watzlawick, Weakland, & Fisch, 1974). The MRI model of problem development suggests that people's attempted solutions, the very ways they hope to improve a given problem, contribute most to the problem's persistence and escalation. Problems begin from some ordinary life difficulty, of which there are usually many in most of our lives. The difficulty may come from an unusual or chance event like the divorce of parents or an unexpected illness. Most often, though, the difficulty is associated with one of the transitions experienced in the course of living and attending school, such as the child's transition from elementary to junior high school.

For a difficulty to turn into a problem, only two conditions need to occur: (1) The difficulty is mishandled (i.e., the solution attempts don't work), and (2) when the difficulty is not resolved, more of the same solution is applied. Then the original difficulty will be worsened, by a vicious-cycle process, eventually becoming a problem whose size and nature bear little resemblance to the original difficulty. *The solution, in essence, is the problem* (Watzlawick et al., 1974).

Based on their assumptions about the problem or how to solve it, people usually try variations of the same solution over and over again. We have frequently witnessed this type of pattern in our work with school problems. This process occurs despite the best intentions of students, parents, and teachers, and despite the fact that the solution attempts are recognized as not helping.

To illustrate how easy it is to get stuck in one solution pattern, consider the following puzzle. The nine dots in the puzzle can be connected using only four straight lines, drawn without taking your pencil off the paper. If you have not seen this puzzle before, take a few minutes to try to solve it.

Now look at the solution below. In trying to solve the puzzle, few people think of extending the straight lines beyond the dots, even though nothing in the instructions prohibits doing so. Most people superimpose an imaginary square on the dots, which precludes solution. By acting on the erroneous assumption that the lines cannot extend beyond the dots, you guarantee two things: frustration and failure. These are the identical outcomes that teachers, parents, and students face when they are stuck in an attempt to resolve a school problem.

Although you may have recognized after just one trial that a solution to the puzzle was impossible, you probably continued to apply the same solution theme over and over again. You may have varied the speed with which you attempted your solution, the frequency of your attempts, and the intensity of your effort, but your solutions were doomed to failure. Being freed from the constraints of the imaginary square expands problem-solving options and makes the nine-dot puzzle solvable. Looking at the relationship between the problem and attempted solutions opens new options for consideration. New directions appear as we discard the blinders of our current solution attempts.

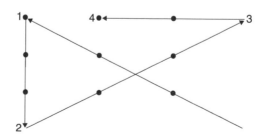

This perspective also applies to what doesn't work in intervention. Students, teachers, and parents consult school practitioners because they are distressed about a particular situation. The practitioner conceptualizes the problem and then intervenes. Upon failure of the intervention, variations of the strategy are applied over and over again. The practitioner may believe he or she is trying different things, but in reality the practitioner is operating from a viewpoint that leads in only one direction—to more of the same. The intervention, in essence, becomes the problem.

Consider Jamie, a 9-year-old boy referred for fighting on the bus. Jamie did not pose a behavioral problem in the classroom and received average grades. He met with the school counselor, who determined that Jamie had self-esteem issues and was having trouble adjusting to his mother's new boyfriend. The counselor recommended a self-esteem group and the removal of privileges for inappropriate bus behavior.

The problem persisted, and Jamie began having behavior problems in the classroom. The teacher referred him for a psychological evaluation, which determined that he was borderline ADHD. A trial of stimulant medication was initiated. Jamie's behavior problems continued. A team meeting was called, which included the counselor, teacher, mother, psychologist, and bus driver. Every intervention was discussed and all agreed that each had merit. However, Jamie's problems persisted.

The counselor suggested that the team start over and discuss the original problem of fighting on the bus. The bus driver described the problem, noting that Jamie is the last stop on the route. The teacher added that most of his classroom problems occurred at the end of the day. The discussion concluded with the bus driver's suggestion that she change her route so that Jamie could be dropped off first instead of last. This suggestion was implemented, and Jamie's bus problem was eliminated. His other problems followed suit. The previous interventions had become an intimate part of the problem. Luckily for Jamie, the team recognized this and decided to "try something different."

But how do we know when we need to try something different? How do we know when we are effective? Traditionally, the effectiveness of intervention (symptom or problem reduction) has been left up to the judgment of the practitioner. We propose something very different: Proof of effectiveness is determined by systematically collecting outcome feedback from students, parents, and teachers, enlisting the client as a full partner in both the intervention and accountability process. Why is this important? Let's consult our first president.

Try Something Different: The Lessons of George Washington

On a cold, blustery December day in 1799, the 67-year-old former president of the United States, George Washington, returned to his mansion from his usual morning ride on the grounds of his Mount Vernon estate. As the day wore on, however, a minor sore throat the president had experienced since his morning ride worsened. By early the next morning, his condition was so grave that a doctor was summoned.

The doctor—along with two other physicians who eventually made it through the snowy weather to Mount Vernon—skillfully and competently administered the accepted intervention of the day. When no results were observed, the three agreed that more of the same treatment was indicated. Several hours and two additional treatments later, the president was dead. The cause of death? Whatever course the disease might have taken, historians agree that the treatment he received while in an already weakened state likely hastened his demise. This intervention, of course, was the accepted "standard of care" for late 18th-century medicine—bloodletting (Flexner, 1974).

While it might be tempting to believe that we have evolved beyond such primitive practices, there is strong evidence that the very same forces that led Washington's physicians to administer (and then readminister) an ineffective (and ultimately lethal) treatment continue to guide the practice of intervention—specifically, an emphasis on the *competence* of service delivery rather than the *effectiveness* of the services delivered. Conventional wisdom suggests that competence engenders, if not equals, effectiveness. As the death of George Washington illustrates, competence is no guarantee of effectiveness. Even ineffective or dangerous interventions can be used competently.

More important, the story shows that having no systematic method for evaluating the outcome of an intervention may create an illusion of success that blinds practitioners to corrective feedback. Consider a study on the qualities of effective practitioners (Hiatt & Hargrave, 1995). Using client self-report and peer ratings, researchers successfully distinguished between least and most effective practitioners (as determined by outcome). In brief, they found that those in the *low* effectiveness group were unaware that they were ineffective. Even worse, they considered themselves as effective as the truly helpful practitioners in the study! In the absence of reliable feedback, practitioners will assume the best and continue to do more of the same intervention with more of the same negative results.

Practitioners can improve effectiveness while simultaneously proving the value of their work by *gathering feedback about the fit and outcome of their services and using that data to inform the next step*. Studies verify that providing practitioners with client-based outcome feedback significantly increases effectiveness (Miller, Duncan, & Hubble, 2004; Whipple et al., 2003). Using client feedback would finally invite the users of our services to be full partners, giving students, parents, and teachers the perspective of the driver's seat instead of the back of the bus—implementing the common factors one client at a time based on each individual's perceptions of the progress and fit of intervention.

Our third guideline, "Try Something Different," also reflects our belief that school practitioners must prove that their work is effective and efficient. As is news to no one, state and federal funders are increasingly cost-conscious and insistent that school practitioners substantiate the effectiveness of their services. In Chapter 4, we advocate routine and systematic assessment of client's perceptions of progress and fit so that intervention may be empirically tailored to the individual needs and characteristics of each client while proving the value of the services. Becoming outcome-informed fits with how most school practitioners prefer to think of themselves—as sensitive to student, parent, and teacher feedback and interested in results.

CONCLUSIONS

Influenced by 40 years of outcome research, we argue in this chapter that the factors common to all intervention models are the mainstay of positive outcomes. Chapter 2 also translated these findings from the empirical research into three pragmatic guidelines:

1. *The Client Knows Best*. Change is spurred most by what's *right* with students, parents, and teachers—their resources, creativity, and relational support networks—not the labels they carry or even the techniques employed by professional helpers. *The client is the filling of the intervention pie.*

2. *Reliance on the Alliance*. The most influence that practitioners can exert on outcome is not based on our theoretical acumen or technical proficiency; rather, our impact lies in building a positive alliance with parents, teachers, and students. Serving the alliance master requires continual monitoring, flexibility, validation, acceptance of client goals, and

honoring the client's theory of change. *We are the crust of the intervention pie.*

3. *If at First You Don't Succeed, Try Something Different.* The MRI taught us that practitioners, like clients, can easily get stuck in the nine-dot problem and continue to employ ineffective strategies. For the field to remain viable and to ensure that we don't fall prey to "more of the same," we suggested that school practitioners systematically include the client in the accountability process and find out sooner rather than later when intervention is not helping; that is, to give students, parents, and teachers a voice that implements the common factors one client at a time while improving effectiveness. Remember George Washington, who might have said, "I wish my practitioners had tried something different!"

CHAPTER 3

♦ ♦ ♦

Assessment 1

Recruiting the Heroic Client

♦

It is easier to discover a deficiency in individuals, in states, and in Providence, than to see their real import and value.
—G. W. F. HEGEL

This is the first of two chapters describing the goals and strategies of assessment. Chapter 3 emphasizes the all-important first interview and translates our first principle of school intervention, "The Client Knows Best," into practical terms for application. Interviewing is not a cold, one-directional process designed to size up students for diagnostic purposes. Rather, interviewing enlists client strengths, resources, and ideas, harvesting change possibilities to build solutions and resolve problems.

This chapter presents two practical formats for interviewing that seek solutions in every contact. Both depend upon rallying the resources of students, parents, and teachers—recruiting the heroic client—for success.

THE HEROIC CLIENT: RECRUITING STRENGTHS, RESOURCES, AND IDEAS

Chapter 2 suggested that school practitioners highlight strengths and abilities rather than deficits and liabilities. Kenny and Molly illustrated

33

that efficient change is accomplished when the practitioner allows student resources and ideas to take center stage. Exploring resources and ideas is especially important with children because their voices often go unheard (Mayall, 2002; Murphy & Duncan, 1997).

Recall that 40 years of outcome data show that clients' strengths and relational supports as well as everything else they bring account for the bulk of change (Asay & Lambert, 1999; Wampold, 2001). The importance of client resources is also supported by the most robust finding in the psychotherapy literature—the so called "dodo bird verdict." The methods work equally well because clients utilize what each method provides to address their problems (Bohart & Tallman, 1999). The dodo bird verdict rings true because the client's abilities to change transcend any differences among models. The data point to the inevitable conclusion that the client is the heroic one in the drama of change (Duncan, Miller, & Sparks, 2004).

Listening for Heroic Stories

School practitioners can cast clients in the role of the primary agents of change by listening for and being curious about heroic stories that reflect the client's role in surmounting obstacles, initiating action, and maintaining positive change. There is no formula here. The key is the attitude the practitioner assumes with regard to the client's inherent resiliencies and abilities. Attending to heroic stories requires a balance between listening empathically to difficulties and being mindful of the strengths that you know are there (Simon, Murphy, & Smith, 2005).

Listening for client strengths does not mean ignoring pain or assuming a cheerleading role. Rather, it requires that the practitioner listen to the whole story: the confusion and the clarity, the suffering and the endurance, the pain and the coping, the desperation and the desire. Listening for heroic stories suggests only that counselors open themselves to the existence of several competing stories about the client's experience.

Diagnosis tells but one story; a problem description tells another. Many other stories of survival and courage simultaneously exist. Although we often think of ourselves and others in black-and-white ways, human beings have multiple sides, depending on who is recounting them and what sides are emphasized. Unfortunately, what we call the Killer D's (e.g., diagnosis, dysfunction, disorder, deficit, disease) have persuaded our profession and many of us to believe in the story of what is wrong with people as the only or best version. It is neither. Listening for heroic stories seeks to identify not what clients need, but rather what they already have that can be used to reach their goals.

Consider 9-year-old Sean. There are stories about a diagnosis of ADHD, classroom problems, and bed-wetting. But other stories of competence and responsibility are also present. As you read the dialogue, consider the following questions:

- What are the obvious and hidden strengths, resources, and resiliencies?
- What are the competing stories of competence?
- What is already present that can be recruited to solve the problems?

Respecting Ms. White's (Sean's teacher) desire to discuss Sean's problems in the classroom and Nicole's (Sean's mom) wish to work on his bed-wetting, the practitioner explored each person's perspective and obtained a detailed story about Sean's problems. The practitioner, while empathic to the impact of these problems, refused to succumb to those stories as the only or truest ones of Sean's life. Instead, the practitioner brought forth competing stories of competence, caring, and courage.

SCHOOL PRACTITIONER (SP): These are some very important concerns about Sean in the classroom and at home. It says a lot about each of you that you are ready to do whatever it takes to improve things. . . . I was wondering, and I would appreciate each of your takes on this, what Sean's life is like separate from these concerns.

SEAN: I like video games!

(*All laugh.*)

NICOLE: Sean has a great love of animals and takes care of all the animals in the house.

SP: Animals?

SEAN: Oh yeah, we have a dog, a cat, an aquarium, and I have guinea pigs in my room.

SP: It takes a lot of responsibility to care for animals.

NICOLE: And he does a very good job of it. I never have to tell him to do anything regarding the animals. He spends a good deal of his free time playing with them and caring for them.

SP: Sean, that's very impressive at your age, to be able to care for other creatures like that . . . to be gentle with them and show them the affection and care they need.

Ms. WHITE: Oh yeah, Sean is really into animals. He just loved the field trip to the Wildlife Preserve. He knew so much that he could have been the tour guide!

SEAN: We saw foxes, soft-shelled turtles, a ferret, and a skunk. . . .

SP: So you saw a lot of animals native to this area.

SEAN: I also saw a squirrel monkey and an owl.

At least three stories have emerged. The story of Sean's bed-wetting and classroom problems is real. But it is not the only one and perhaps not the most reflective of his identity. There is another story of a remarkably responsible boy who loves animals, and yet another unexplored story of a boy who likes video games. Clients' heroic stories pave the way for change by showcasing abilities and making them available for use. You might be thinking that video game competence is irrelevant and provides few resources to harness for change. Consider the following excerpt from a conversation between Sean and the school practitioner.

SP: So your teacher and your mom brought lots of different things to talk about. What is the most important thing for you?

SEAN: The pee problem. . . . I can't stay over at my friends' houses.

SP: Okay, that makes sense. So you mentioned you really like to play video games. What is your favorite game?

SEAN: Super Mario.

SP: Okay, I know that one. What's the name of the bad guy, the guy. . .

SEAN: The guy that looks like a rock and breathes fire, the guy that stomps on people, that's Bowser. People think he is a dragon, but he is a turtle.

SP: Yeah, Bowser. I am thinking that he is kinda like this pee problem.

SEAN: And you have to break it up.

SP: And you have to break it up. Exactly! So, this pee monster is kinda like Bowser and playing against Mario. You know, when you first play those games, you are not very good at it.

SEAN: Yeah.

SP: And after you play a while, you learn what you have to do to defeat the dragon or monster.

SEAN: Yeah, when I was fighting the frosty dragon, when I got to the last part I had to use my fire power so I could melt all the ice in my way and he was breaking the floor, the dragon, and it was made out of ice and he fell and fell. But then one time, I started racing before him and melting all the ice and when he got very low I jumped over him. That's his weakness.

SP: I wonder what the weakness of the pee dragon is.

SEAN: I don't know. But I know about the frosty dragon. In his mouth he has this power orb, and when you find it you can defeat him.

SP: You're really good at defeating these monsters and dragons.

SEAN: Yeah and I had a problem with the next one because he has a shield and I wasn't sure where his weakness was. But I finally found that his weakness is his head and when you hit him, his power shield comes down. Everything has a weakness.

SP: Everything has a weakness is exactly right. It's just learning what that weakness is, so you can defeat that monster. . . . I wonder what kind of tools or weapons you would need to go to bed with. You know, sometimes in Mario, you got the hat that will give you wings.

SEAN: Yeah, you have to jump three times and look up, then they bring you up to a special stage and you reach the hat, there's like all these coins and you can get a star if you get them all, and then you stomp on it and you can fly.

SP: Yeah, so I wonder what kind of special things you need to defeat the pee monster. Let's see . . .

SEAN: Well, the water is a trap. It's like a big giant blob that when you drink it, it gets all over your body and you get stuck in it, and then the pee monster makes you pee.

SP: That's exactly right, that's incredible. I think you are really onto something with that! Okay, one of the things you need to defeat the pee monster is to . . .

SEAN: Not get near water.

(Sean and the practitioner discuss strategies for watching his fluid intake at night before bed.)

SP: To help you defeat the pee monster, would you be willing to draw a picture of him so we could keep an eye on him, learn his weaknesses, and keep track of the nights you defeat him?

SEAN: Yeah and I could draw a picture of me defeating him.

SP: Great! That might help us come up with other tools too. But you really came up with a good one already, the water thing. Any other kind of special weapons you would need against the pee monster?

SEAN: Maybe some other powers because he is clever monster.

SP: He's a pretty clever monster. But I am pretty sure you are even cleverer than he is.

SEAN: Yeah.

Sean's competence at video games was recruited to help the school practitioner discuss the bed-wetting problem with Sean as well as possible strategies to defeat the pee monster.

School professionals may also inquire more directly about strengths and heroic stories. Table 3.1 provides several possibilities. One particularly interesting question is "Who in your life wouldn't be surprised to see you stand up to these situations and prevail?" Sometimes, others appreciate clients for the treasures they are when they themselves have trouble seeing it. Returning to Sean:

SP: Who wouldn't be surprised to see you defeat the pee monster and the classroom problems?

SEAN: My grandma—she always tells me I can do anything I set my mind to.

SP: What would she tell me about you that would convince me that she was right about thinking you could do it?

SEAN: She would tell about last summer when she got sick and I was staying with her. I got up and then I couldn't wake her up. I shook and shook her but she wouldn't open her eyes. I tried calling my

TABLE 3.1. Questions to Elicit Strengths and Heroic Stories

- What are the traits, qualities, and characteristics that describe you when you are at your very best? What were you doing when these aspects became apparent to you?

- What kind of person do these aspects describe? Or, what kind of person do these aspects show an aspiration toward?

- What are the traits, qualities, and characteristics that others would describe in you when you are at your very best? What were you doing when they noticed these aspects in you?

- What kind of person do these aspects describe? Or, what kind of person do these aspects show an aspiration toward?

- Who was the first person to tell you that he or she noticed the best of you in action? What were you doing when this person noticed these aspects?

- Who was the last person to tell you that he or she noticed the best of you in action? What were you doing when this person noticed these aspects?

- Who in your life wouldn't be surprised to see you stand up to these situations and prevail? What experiences would they draw upon to make these conclusions about you? What stories about "the real you" would they tell?

- When I am at my very best, I am _____.

---

mom but she was in with the doctor and had her cell phone off. Then I called 911 and they took my grandma to the hospital. They said that saved her life. So Grandma always says that if I figured all that out, I could figure out anything.

SP: Wow, I am really convinced. What kind of person does something that smart and brave?

SEAN: I don't know. . . . I guess someone that can handle stuff, and I love my grandma a whole bunch.

(*The school practitioner reconvenes with Ms. White and Nicole.*)

SP: Sean told me how he saved his grandma last summer. Did you know about that, Ms. White?

MS. WHITE: No, I didn't. What happened?

NICOLE: Oh, yeah, Sean really did a great thing . . . (*Tells the story while Sean beams with pride.*)

SP: Sounds like we have a real live hero on our hands. What courage and presence of mind it took to call 911. So, in addition to being the kind of kid you can count on in a pinch, I was thinking that Sean also is unusually responsible in taking care of the animals. Remembering all the things that have to be done and then doing them speaks to a level of maturity that is pretty impressive. And (*turning to Sean*) you are really good at video games! You know all the ins and outs—the strategies about getting power, and how you can take a small step and that gives you a little more power. Is that how it works? If you could make one success, it gives you more power. Is that right?

SEAN: If you make one success, you are going to get more successes.

SP: So you don't get, like, really strong and powerful right away?

SEAN: Yeah, you have to, like, do the game over and over. You have to keep playing to get good and go to the next level.

SP: Okay, so if you are going to go after this pee monster, it sounds like your mom has done a lot of things to help you with that, and I am just wondering what you think about what your mom could do to help you, or is this something you have to do on your own?

SEAN: I think I have to do something on my own because I can't keep on depending on my mom all my life. [After all, Sean is 9 years old!]

SP: I really admire that you want to accomplish this on your own. (*to Nicole*) You have done a lot to give him what he needs to resolve this and I really think you are on the right track. [An earlier discussion detailed a variety of strategies for dealing with both homework and the bed-wetting.] Sean is a great kid. You have done so well with him.

NICOLE: Thanks! Yes, he is a loving child and I am proud of him.

SP: He's got some great ideas on dealing with this and I asked him to . . .

SEAN: Draw a picture.

SP: Draw a picture of the pee monster because we have to get an idea of what this guy looks like so that Sean can find his weaknesses and figure out what he needs to do to defeat the pee monster. Sean already has some good ideas and is going to think about that more, but the first thing we talked about was drawing a picture so we could start visualizing what this monster looks like, so then he could visualize defeating the monster.

The practitioner reinforced Sean's competencies, and it rang true for Nicole. Sean's story of classroom problems and bed-wetting was real, but it was not the only one. An additional story of responsibility, love, and competence also emerged, which formed the foundation for change. Note how a focus on Sean's more heroic aspects resulted in his enthusiasm for problem resolution and desire to take responsibility. Sean returned with his drawing and reported that he had defeated the pee monster on several occasions. His teacher also reported successes in the classroom, which fueled further changes, just as Sean predicted. Once a change was noted, the school practitioner sought to empower the changes.

Empowering Change

Whether change begins before or during intervention, whether it results from the client's own actions or by happenstance, a crucial step in empowering change is helping clients see any gains as a consequence of their own efforts and as part of an emerging heroic story of a new identity. A cardinal consideration is perception: clients' perception of the relationship between their own efforts and the occurrence of change, and the meaning of it in the context of their lives. At the least, it is important that clients come to view the change as resulting from something they did and can repeat in the future.

Practitioners can express curiosity about the client's role in any changes that occur and ask questions or make direct statements that presuppose client involvement in the resulting change (Murphy, in press; Walter & Peller, 1992).

> "Wait a second. You did what? Tell me more about that. How did you know to do what you did? That was thoughtful. What is it about you that helped you to do what you did? What did you learn about yourself?"

Even if clients resolutely attribute change to luck, fate, the acumen of the practitioner, or a medication, they can still be asked to consider in detail: (1) how they adopted the change in their lives, (2) what they did to use the changes to their benefit, (3) what they will do in the future to ensure that their gains remain in place, and (4) how the changes reflect new chapters in their lives.

Helping students, parents, and teachers take credit for steps in the right direction casts them in their rightful roles as the main characters in their stories of change. The school practitioner shines a spotlight on any accomplishments and requests that the client take a bow for his or her creativity, courage, and good ideas. Basking in the limelight of success keeps the positive performances coming. Returning to Sean:

SP: Looks like you really are showing that pee monster who's boss. How are you putting him in his place?

SEAN: I don't know, just not drinking water after supper and going to the bathroom a lot at night.

SP: Man, that's great. You really figured out what you needed to do. How do you think you did that?

SEAN: I guess I really wanted to stay over at friends' houses. . . . I did that for the first time last weekend.

SP: Terrific. What do you think this says about what kind of kid you are?

SEAN: That I am how my grandma says . . . that I can figure things out.

SP: Your grandma is a smart lady!

Another way to showcase gains as arising from client efforts is to make "before and after" distinctions. The idea is to encourage reflection and distinguish between the way things were *before* the change, and how things are now, *after* the change. This invites clients to explore the significance of their actions and tell a different story about their life—one of triumph, enlightenment, and tenacity. The change itself is a land-mark on the landscape of the client's life, and something that he or she can always point to as the place in the journey where a different path was taken. At its best, fleshing out all the nuances of success creates a newfound identity of wisdom and competence gained from the school of hard knocks.

Questions that empower change with students, parents, and teachers:

- How did you decide that now was the time for action?
- What insights have you gained from your life that you were finally able to put into action?

- What insights have you gained from this change that will help you in the future?
- What does this say about you, the kind of person you are, that you made these changes at this time?
- Who in your past would not be surprised to see you making these changes?
- How did you do it? How will you maintain the gains you have made?
- How are you different now that you have realized this change?

For example, the school practitioner followed up with Ms. White:

SP: Looks like you really have gotten over the hump with Sean in the classroom. How were you able to turn him around?

MS. WHITE: Well, Sean did a lot too. He is really a sweet kid. I think I was a bit on the trigger-happy side before I had a chance to really think this through.

SP: What do you mean?

MS. WHITE: Well, I think I was kind of breathing down Sean's neck a bit too much and perhaps overbearing, if you know what I mean. I've learned that wasn't a good strategy with him, although it is with some of the other kids who have attention problems. I've learned that ignoring the little stuff and refocusing him with our code words seems to be helping.

SP: Sounds like you were open to learning from a trial-and-error process with Sean and that you applied something that has really worked. Tell me more about the refocusing.

MS. WHITE: It really is kind of a hoot. Because of Sean's love of animals, he and I developed code words for when I want him to pay attention to things. When I want him to get to work, I say "beaver," as in busy as a beaver, and when I say "mouse," it means I want him to be quiet as a mouse. He smiles almost every time I say one of our animal code words, but it seems to refocus him most of the time. If he is really kinda all over the place, I say squirrel, as in he is acting squirrelly. (*Both laugh.*)

SP: This is priceless. Your creativity is refreshing. How did you come to this insight about teaching?

MS. WHITE: This is how I want to be as a teacher. This is the kind of teacher I admire most. The more I thought about Sean and how he used his drawing to defeat that pee monster (*laughs*), the more I thought that I was a bit on the too serious side of things in my approach to behavior problems in the classroom. I don't know, I think that I have always been pretty good at dealing with kids, but I like how this is going and think it has been a good thing for me to think about.

SP: I think you are already that teacher you aspire to be.

It is also helpful to encourage clients to reward themselves for their changes by doing something special to punctuate and celebrate successes. It doesn't matter what it is—just something that adds an exclamation point to the fact that they did something very positive. Moreover, to further highlight the accomplishments, we also recommend that clients do something that symbolizes the change as a turning point—a token or milestone to serve as a constant reminder that the client took the initiative and did not condemn him- or herself to a less fulfilling existence. This concrete indication, marking the beginning of something new and better, could be anything from making a collage to getting a puppy, from doing volunteer work to writing poetry. It doesn't matter what it is. It only needs to have meaning to the client. Ms. White rewarded herself and Sean with additional class field trips to museums and animal sanctuaries.

HARVESTING CHANGE POSSIBILITIES

If you are like many people, you prefer to have something you can hold on to when you are on unfamiliar ground, such as when you meet with students, parents, and teachers for the first time to address a problem. Models of interviewing or formats of questions can provide some structure to help us when we feel lost in the sea of information that clients give us. These formats share the common ideal that students, parents, and teachers—no matter how troubled they are, no matter how distressing their situation, no matter how hopeless they feel—can be in a different place by the end of your conversation with them: not fixed or cured, but no longer reading their story from the section titled "Future Dismal, Prospects Bleak." By virtue of the dynamic moment-to-moment conversational exchange that we call interviewing, the possibility of a better future can be first imagined, and then actualized. Possibility enters the room like fresh air from an open window after a long winter season; everyone breathes a little easier and the business of change is well under way.

The next two sections detail two interviewing formats for harvesting possibilities for change: *solution building* and *problem busting*. These formats need not be rigidly applied and can be integrated at will, but both depend on the recruited strengths of students, parents, and teachers. One caveat: The problem with great ideas is that they can fall prey to someone turning them into a model that *should* be used across situations. No model can take precedence over a client's preferences or is more important than the alliance.

Solution Building

Solution-focused therapy (Berg & Miller, 1992; de Shazer, 1985) proposed the revolutionary idea that the solution to the problem does not necessarily have any relationship to the problem. Steve de Shazer, one of the pioneers of this approach, tells the story of a Japanese farmer working in the rice fields high above a coastal village who saw a tidal wave rapidly approaching. The villagers could not have heard her had she yelled to them, nor did she have time to run to the village to warn them. She set the rice on fire. When the villagers rushed to save the vital crop, they were spared certain death from the tidal wave.

There is no relationship between the impending doom of the tidal wave (the problem) and setting the rice fields on fire (the solution). The solution can occur without knowing or even talking about the problem. This idea releases you from the necessary hunt for the problem and its causes, allowing you to explore how the resources of the client can be put to work. It frees you up to ask about *exceptions*—times when the problem doesn't occur or occurs less often or intensely. Exploring exceptions showcases client competencies and engages clients in the search of their own experiences for solutions.

The Three E's of Solution Building

Heraclites is often credited with saying that nothing is permanent but change. Unlike diagnoses—static characterizations connoting a measure of constancy—the severity and frequency of problems are in flux. With or without prompting, clients can describe these changes—the ebb and flow of the problem's presence and ascendancy in their daily affairs. These reported changes and seemingly unrelated, serendipitous events provide powerful opportunities for new heroic stories to be told.

Shining a spotlight on exceptions illuminates existing client resources, allowing their enlistment. To begin, school practitioners need only to believe, like Heraclites, in the certainty of change. The following illustrates a three-step method of utilizing exceptions: *eliciting, elaborating, and expanding.*

STEP 1: ELICITING THE EXCEPTION

An exception can be considered a small success in daily life. From a practical standpoint, it is often easier to increase existing successes, no matter how small, than to eliminate a problem. Sometimes a dogged pursuit of the problem blinds us to solution opportunities that are right under our nose. Even in seemingly dismal situations, exceptions usually can be discovered. For example, the student who reportedly "disrupts class constantly" and "never does any schoolwork" has probably behaved appropriately in class at *one time* or another, and has completed *some* assignment along the way. It is important to be alert to the verbal cues of exceptions. Statements such as "failing everything *except* science" or "has completed work *only once* this week" provide starting points for building upon what a student and others are already doing effectively.

It is often necessary to ask questions to elicit exceptions:

- When is the problem absent or less noticeable during the school day?
- What is happening at school that you want to see continue happening?
- What changes have occurred since making this appointment?

Similarly, should the client return for additional visits, attention can be directed to changes taking place between meetings. For example, the practitioner can amplify any references the client makes to between-visit improvement or positive events not directly related to the client's stated concerns. In the opening moments, the practitioner can ask the clients about what changes have occurred since his or her last visit. The simplest question comes in this form: "What is different?" or "What is better?" Such an inquiry, when used with sensitivity to the client's acceptance, focuses both on change and on the client's contribution in bringing it about. The client's experience of change figures prominently in the approach to outcome management discussed in Chapter 4.

These instances of liberation from the problem form the foundation for building solutions because *somehow the client is already solving the problem.* There is part of the client that is dealing with the problem differently, even if he or she is initially unaware of it. Sometimes just recognizing the problem's inability to control one's life 24/7 can inspire insights about the problem and ideas for further changes.

Consider 15-year-old Ellen, who, because of many abusive experiences, often superficially cuts herself on her arms to relieve emotional pain. After noting exceptions to her cutting, the practitioner suggested that there was a part of her—the master at the control panel—that pushed the right buttons and controlled the cutting. The task, the school practitioner intimated, was to learn more about *how* she was able to do it. Ellen returned and ended her counseling. She reported that the more she considered herself the master at the control panel, the more she realized that she could overcome the cutting. And she did. Although not all situations will resolve as quickly as Ellen's, clients' awareness of their ability to overthrow the problem, even for a short time, can lead to further insurrections and a revolution of change.

It is also possible to elicit exceptions through the suggestion of tasks. The so-called "first-session formula tasks" (de Shazer, 1985) are designed to capitalize on the constancy of change and encourage clients to notice exceptions:

- Between now and the next time we get together, note the things in your life (or in another person, or in your relationship with so and so, or in this specific situation, etc.) that you would like to see continue.
- Pay attention to the times you are able to overcome the temptation to interrupt your teacher (or whatever the problem is).
- Observe when the problem isn't occurring or is just a little better, and how you are able to make it that way.

Consider Isabel and Jorge. They were at their wits' end because their 13-year-old daughter, Alina, burst into tears and stormed out after an argument about a bad grade. This wasn't the first time. These all too familiar scenes, Alina's emotional outbursts in response to almost everything, were the cause of increasing alarm to her parents. Jorge was particularly concerned about the long-term consequences of Alina's inability to control her emotions. He feared that these tirades would hurt her chances in life and that she would be doomed if she kept responding so strongly to life's inevitable ups and downs.

Isabel phoned the school practitioner, and he suggested that the parents note what they would like to see continue in Alina. Isabel especially liked the idea because she thought that things had just gotten too negative around the house. They told Alina about the task and that they would report their findings back to her.

A couple of weeks later, after consulting the practitioner about the next step, Isabel, Jorge, and Alina got together after dinner and discussed what they had seen during the observation period. Despite the seeming constancy of the problems, Isabel and Jorge were able to share a long list of positive events and attributes. Alina was "caught" being more communicative, more cooperative, and able to keep her emotions in check. We will follow this family throughout our discussion of the three E's to solution building.

Finally, when fishing for exceptions, it can also be helpful to be curious about *anything* in the client's life that is helpful or going well. This way of thinking seeks to amplify what works in order to minimize what doesn't. Typically, when there is a problem, we want to attack it directly. That's okay, but it is not the only way to make things better. You can also ignore the problem completely and focus instead on increasing those things in the client's life that enhance feelings of competence, confidence, or self-esteem. Whether seeking out a trusted friend or family member, working out or taking a walk, purchasing a book or tape, attending church or a mutual-help group, or going to a movie or a concert, important clues to gaining relief from the problem can occur by taking a broader perspective beyond just exceptions to the problem. Increasing these aspects can turn the tables on a problem, making it shrink to a shadow of its former self.

For example, 14-year-old Tony was just about climbing out of his skin when he came to see the school counselor. After he shared how the anxiety attacks tormented every waking minute, as well as all his frustrated attempts to do something about them (from drugs to therapy to you name it), the counselor asked Tony about exceptions. First, Tony couldn't identify any times without the anxiety. Then the counselor asked him what was going well in his life, and he immediately responded that his triathlon training was going great. The counselor learned of all the positives that Tony's participation in this rigorous sport brought to him, especially the races themselves. Tony felt invincible during the thrill of competition regardless of how he placed. As the conversation unfolded, Tony intimated that he was only able to participate in a race every 3 months because most of the races were not local. As the discussion concluded, Tony noted that the triathlon contests were huge exceptions to his anxiety and panic attack problem. He just didn't think about the problem when a race was imminent. The school counselor asked Tony if there was any way he could enter more triathlon events.

Tony was able to find races in cities where he could travel with his parents' help. When he was unable to find enough events to compete in at least monthly, Tony joined the triathlon organization that scheduled the races. The anxiety, while still present, receded into the background. Tony was able to turn the tables on his anxiety; he amplified what was going well to diminish what was not. Some might second-guess Tony's success and suggest that he didn't really deal with the "underlying" problem, but Tony didn't mind.

To search for exceptions in other areas of life, ask these questions:

- Who or what is helpful or going well in your life?
- What do you seek out for even a small measure of comfort?
- What things are happening that you would like to see continue?
- What do you enjoy doing outside of school?
- What are you good at?

STEP 2: ELABORATING THE EXCEPTION

Once identified, the exception is elaborated upon by inquiring about related features and circumstances. Elaborating exceptions requires the practitioner to unfold the noted difference and allow the client to fully appreciate its significance. This helps to link the positive change to the client's own behavior, thus highlighting the change as an instance of self-healing and perhaps the beginning of an important new chapter.

The particulars about the exception form the basis for solutions. Elaborating the exception asks, "How did it happen?" and requires you to ask "who, what, when, where, and why" questions about the noted instance of life without the problem to ferret out all its specifics.

For example, a student who reportedly misbehaves in all classes except math might be asked the following questions:

- In what ways is your math class/teacher different from other classes/teachers?
- Where do you sit in math class?
- How would you rate your interest in math relative to other classes?

Questions to parents and teachers may include the following:

- Who is around when things seem to go smoother at home?
- What do you do or say differently when you and the student are getting along better?
- How is it that things go better in math than the other classes?
- What was happening at those times? What do you think you were doing to help that along? What would you need to do (or what would need to happen) for you to experience more of that?
- In what ways is it different, more bearable, or less noticeable?
- Who is involved when things are different? Where did the difference happen?
- How do you explain the exception? How did you make it happen?
- If your friend, family, or significant other were here, what would they say is different about you during times when the problem is not happening?

Ask parents and teachers to keep track of everything that is helpful in any way—even if it appears insignificant.

Consider a parent and teenager who complain of ongoing fights. In response to an observation task, they report that they do not argue when they go to the movies. Questions about how they miraculously achieve harmony in these circumstances may include the following: Why do you think things go so smoothly at the movies? What do you do or say differently when you are getting along better? What is it about going to the movies that brings out your best? Is there a particular kind of movie that seems to have this effect? Resist the tendency to gloss over successes or any differences in the problem, and, instead, doggedly pursue the exception until all the elaboration is "chewed" out of it. For example, some practitioners might diminish the preceding exception to the parent and teenagers fighting because it occurred at the movies where they didn't have to talk to each other. Nothing could be further from the truth. They talked on the way to the movies, while parking the car and walking to the theater, at the concession stand, while waiting for the movie to start, and so on. There were plenty of opportunities for a fight to start, but it didn't. Somehow, something about the parent and child and the movies mixed together made something good happen—an instance of the problem not occurring. Don't underestimate any exception to the problem! Take exceptions seriously and elaborate them as much as possible.

Following completion of the "note what you would like to see continue" task, Jorge and Isabel shared the positive things they noticed with Alina. Elaborating on those exceptions led to new directions. When detailing these exceptions to Alina's emotional outbursts and what each person did to make them happen, Jorge concluded that his "backing off" and appreciating Alina's strengths seemed to have a big impact on things going better around the house. Everyone agreed. Alina observed that she got what she wanted a lot more when she had a friendly attitude and made attempts to talk with her parents about everyday stuff rather than only confronting them when she was mad. Finally, Isabel observed that when a disagreement did occur, the whole family seemed to take it in stride rather than blowing it up to a huge problem. Everyone seemed to be trying just a little bit harder to get along.

Such elaborations paint a vivid picture of the times of liberation from the problem and identify exactly the type of canvas, paint color, and brush size that clients will need to replicate similar pictures in the future. Describing all the details shows you how to repeat and expand successes.

STEP 3: EXPANDING THE EXCEPTION

Following the identification of an exception and its elaboration, the task shifts to expanding the exception (1) to other contexts or (2) to a greater frequency. As an example of expanding to other contexts, consider the student who misbehaved in all but one class. When it was discovered that this was the only class in which she did not sit next to good friends, her other teachers changed seating arrangements, with positive results.

This step simply encourages the student, parent, or teacher to do "more of" what is already working. For example, a student complained of ongoing arguments with his stepfather. When asked to describe times when they got along better, he mentioned that they enjoyed talking about sports, especially tennis and baseball. To expand this exception, the student was encouraged to initiate a discussion shortly after arriving home from school each day about tennis or baseball, before any arguments could occur. They noticed immediate improvement, highlighting the idea that sometimes the best way to solve problems is to amplify what is already working. But they went even further by making a rule that each person had to use sports metaphors in any conflict that might arise. Communication problems were discussed as "missed signals" between a third base coach and a batter in baseball, while disagreements were seen as "line disputes" between a tennis player and the line judge. Sometimes the metaphors were so silly that they forgot what they were arguing about. One success often builds on another, and enhances everyone's creativity in resolving problems.

Amplify or do more of what's working by asking these questions:

- How can you do more of what you are doing that is helpful?
- How can you do more of what is going right in your life?
- What will it take to continue this strategy?

Isabel, Jorge, and Alina decided to continue to notice the good things about Alina and elaborate those items into suggestions for family behavior. The family compiled a list of the things that proved helpful and posted it on the refrigerator.

The practitioner assisted the family in maintaining and empowering desired changes. Isabel and Jorge attributed the changes in Alina and overall family harmony to their efforts at backing off and appreciating her strengths. But on further reflection with the school practitioner, another, more profound change was noted. As Jorge thought about the "before-and-after" experiences with Alina, he noticed that he became more concerned about his relationship with his daughter. Jorge realized that he often compared Alina to her more popular sisters and had not noticed what he had come to deeply respect in her. Alina was not swept away by the urge to be popular, to wear the right clothes, or to listen to the right music. She was far more interested in being actively involved in what was going on in the world and invested in making it a better place.

Jorge looked back at the situation with Alina and the changes he made, and concluded that it enabled him to feel better about himself as a parent. He treasured this before-and-after distinction, and empowered it by scheduling a "political night" with Alina to discuss world events. The spirited debates that ensued forever bonded the father and daughter in ways that neither could have predicted nor could ever forget.

THE BOTTOM LINE OF SOLUTION BUILDING

The three-E method of building solutions can be reduced to a few questions and actions: "When are the times clients have been able to resist giving in to talking in class, overeating, fear, arguing, arriving late, depression, etc.?" When those times are noted, next ask: "How was he or she able to do this at this time?" Also make note of what the client did specifically to accomplish this each time. Encourage more of what the client did, in order to continue keeping the problem at arm's length, if not off the radar altogether. Finally, ask, "What does the client's ability to stand up to the problem tell you about who he or she is as a person and what he or she is capable of?" "Who else is aware of these traits?" "How can I invite others to recognize and celebrate these special attributes?" Encourage clients to give themselves a special treat (party, bubble bath, box of chocolates, movie ticket, fishing trip, day at the beach, etc.) to reward themselves for even small victories over the problem.

Solution Building with Beth and Jermaine

Jermaine, age 8, was referred by his special education teacher, Beth, for frequent screaming in class, minimal work completion, and aggressive behaviors. A review of the records indicated a highly problematic school and family history. Jermaine was reportedly a "crack baby." His mother was deceased and father was in prison. He lived with his grandmother. He was enrolled in a special education program for students with mild mental disabilities.

Since Jermaine's teacher, Beth, initiated the referral, she was approached first regarding her perceptions of the situation and related goals. As is most often the case with a teacher referral, the teacher is the real customer for change—the one most motivated to see change occur. Beth was no exception. The school practitioner explored her frame of reference about Jermaine and what she thought would help. Beth thought that everything possible had been done, and was feeling hopeless and demoralized. The practitioner validated Beth's frustration. He complimented her for all she had done for Jermaine and for her willingness to seek help again. Beth appreciated recognition of all her hard work, as well as her values about teaching.

The following illustrates *eliciting* and *elaborating* exceptions:

SP: These kids are very lucky to have you. You have really done a lot. When have the problems with Jermaine been better?

BETH: Thanks . . . sometimes it's real hard. There was one week, early in the year, that was better. He settled down, didn't hardly yell, stayed on task, and was not near as disruptive.

SP: What was that all about?

BETH: Well, his aunt was visiting his grandmother. His grandmother just doesn't seem to have any control over him. She will give him anything to stop his screaming at home. We have tried so many things to involve her in making things better, but we have been unable to get her to follow through. For example, we tried to get her to make T.V. contingent upon our token economy here. Anyway, we asked Jermaine why he was getting his work done and he said that his aunt was visiting, to help his grandma out because she was sick. He said that she made him do it.

SP: That's very interesting. I wonder how she made him do it.

BETH: Jermaine's aunt brought him to school one day that week and I had a chance to talk to her. She said when Jermaine screamed, she whupped him (*laughs*). She also said she doesn't put up with any nonsense from him.

SP: It sounds like his aunt puts the fear in him.

BETH: Yeah, she does, but Jermaine loves her dearly. He was falling all over himself to please her and show her off that day she was here.

SP: His aunt seems to have some special influence. I was also noticing in his record that he did better last year. Referrals seemed to diminish as the year progressed. Can you make any sense of that?

BETH: Well, it's funny, his teacher from last year, he adores her. Whenever Mrs. K visits him, he swoons and carries on like you wouldn't believe. His behavior is much less disruptive. Sometimes she has lunch with him.

SP: How is he on those days?

BETH: He's better. Yeah, he's better.

The discussion began with Beth recounting all the different ways she attempted to help Jermaine. The practitioner listened empathically and complimented Beth's successes with the other kids in the class, who the practitioner recognized from referrals in previous years. Beth was an experienced and compassionate teacher who clearly was an expert at dealing with challenging students.

The practitioner allowed Beth to describe her frustrations and validated both her competence and her exasperation. He explored for exceptions and the ensuing discussion revealed the discovery of two notable instances of improved behavior. Jermaine's behavior was influenced positively by contact with both his aunt and his former teacher. Notice how the exceptions evolved directly from Beth's experience. Note also how the exceptions, although dramatic, were overlooked. The task now shifted to *expanding* these exceptions and amplifying their impact in Jermaine's day-to-day life.

SP: I really think you are on to something here. We know what can help, but how can we make it help more consistently?

BETH: I have some ideas about that (*sounding energized*). I can call his aunt and see if she can somehow become part of his daily homework routine. Maybe even if it is only by phone, it could help.

SP: That's a great idea. What about his former teacher?

BETH: I was thinking we could involve her in our daily token economy. I'm sure she will be willing. If Jermaine achieves green level, or essentially doesn't scream and does his work, maybe Mrs. K can visit him briefly during her study period. Perhaps also, if Jermaine maintains improvement all week, then he can have lunch with her.

SP: Sounds great. That's really a creative way to address this situation with Jermaine.

BETH: Thanks. This has really given me hope. Thank you very much. I felt so helpless with him.

Beth implemented her plan and was successful at involving both Jermaine's aunt and his previous teacher. Jermaine's behavior and academic performance improved. The task now shifted to *empowering* Jermaine's progress.

SP: Sounds like things are really going better. Now that some time has passed, how do you account for the changes?

BETH: I think that involving the aunt was the big thing.

SP: How were you able to pull that off?

BETH: Well, I just called her and expressed my frustrations and honestly pleaded with her to help (*laughs*), given how she seemed to be able to influence Jermaine in such a positive way. The best thing to come out of it, though, is Jermaine's grandmother seems to be more involved too.

SP: How so?

BETH: She is signing his work and calling me more often. I am developing a good rapport with her. What a job she took on, after raising four kids on her own. You got to admire that. I think I was giving her a bum rap.

SP: I'm really impressed how you turned this situation around, especially how you were able to persuade the aunt to monitor the homework, and also how you have made inroads with Jermaine's grandmother as well.

BETH: I think that Jermaine has figured out that there is no escape (*laughs*). We got him covered at all ends. His aunt also wants me to call her during the day if Jermaine is having a bad day. Guess what, I have only called one time! And you know what else? I learned something about me too. Before the situation started to turn, as bad as I hate to say it, I was counting Jermaine out. I was thinking of him in terms of the labels that are in his file, even though I know better than that. I am not going to let that happen because that flies in the face of all the reasons I got into this kind of teaching. Jermaine and this process with him helped me re-remember why I am a special education teacher.

SP: I wonder if there is a way you can reward yourself for all your hard work with Jermaine, and perhaps even commemorate how you re-remembered something so important to your identity as a teacher.

BETH: Good question. I could get an afternoon off and get to that art exhibit I've wanted to attend. And, you know, I am going to e-mail my mentor from graduate school and ask her to send me a picture to put up in my classroom. That will signify my recommitment to giving these kids the best shot they can have. . . .

Everything about the intervention came from the client. Beth successfully applied her noted exceptions to Jermaine's problems and made a significant impact. The practitioner explored what Beth knew, validated her competence, and imbued the process with hope by having faith in her abilities to improve Jermaine's behavior.

Problem Busting

Over 30 years ago, researchers and clinicians at the Mental Research Institute (MRI) discovered that the relationship between a problem and attempted solutions provided a unique vantage point for problem solving. They concluded that because of the intimate connection between the solution and the problem, one only needs to change the solution to impact the problem regardless of how long the problem has been around.

This idea, that the solution is the problem, is a gem because it normalizes the experience of problems and frees intervention from the encumbrances of the Killer D's. The task is merely to encourage the client to change the way the problem is approached. This simple idea translates to three easy steps that explore student, parent, and teacher experiences; recognize the patterns involved in problems; and encourage fresh strategies to forge new directions.

Pat and Ann illustrate the key elements of a problem-busting first interview (Fisch et al., 1982). Pat, a 37-year-old full-time mother of two, was referred by the principal for a conference with the school practitioner. She had worked her way through the administration at the school, ruffling feathers along the way with her ardent concerns about her 9-year-old daughter Ann's "depression." The problem was that no one shared her concerns. Ann was a hard-working and well-behaved student according to her teacher. Everyone believed Ann to be remarkably well adjusted, despite a mother who was described as a "certifiable nut" and a "loose cannon waiting to go off."

Pat was an interesting character, full of extremes. She was charming and impeccably dressed, and spoke in a boisterous manner, emphasizing her points with sweeping gestures and intense eye contact. Ann looked like any 9-year-old but, predictably enough, wore an embarrassed expression that said she wanted to be somewhere else. She slumped in the chair and didn't look up as her mother opened the meeting by saying, "Ann is so depressed."

Pointing to her daughter, she said, "She complains about being bored and mopes around." She gestured broadly with her hands and continued, "I'm depressed, and I know that I have a chemical imbalance and will need to take antidepressants the rest of my life. I also take antipsychotics, because I had a psychotic break right after Ann was born—tried to kill myself and the whole nine yards. My mother is also depressed and takes antidepressants. My doctor told me it was genetic, and I'm sure that Ann is just like my mother and me and probably needs to be on medication, too."

Ann's teacher, assistant principal, and principal had already attempted to persuade Pat that nothing was wrong. Recall our discussion of the alliance. Pat perceived these well-intended efforts as belittling Ann's problems and subtly indicting Pat's competence as a parent. Challenging Pat and her genetic-depression view only would have attached the school practitioner to the conga line of failure. Instead, the practitioner validated Pat's view of her daughter's genetic depression and conducted a problem-busting interview to harvest change possibilities.

Step 1: Detailing the Problem

It is the client's view of the problem that lays the foundation for everything that follows. The first step is a *concrete, action-oriented* answer to the MRI question, "Who is doing what that presents a problem, to whom, and how does such behavior constitute a problem?" Answering this question enables you to identify the first crucial part of the problem–solution cycle. What you want to know is what each individual involved in the problem is specifically saying and doing in *performing* the problem, rather than relying on general statements or abstract explanations. For example, saying that someone is depressed doesn't really say much about that person's unique experience. Depression can have as many different expressions as there are people. What you want to consider is how the person "does" the depression: how it actually looks, sounds, and acts. Thinking of examples is often the best way to get specifics—particular instances of the problem will help describe it in detail and reveal how it impacts the client and others. Questions to obtain information about the problem follow:

- Can you describe a recent example of the problem?
- If I were a fly on the wall, what would I see?
- If I recorded the problem on a video camera, what would I see and hear?
- What happens first? Then what happens? Then what?
- How often does it occur? How long does it last?
- Who is usually around when it happens?
- What are they doing or saying?
- What stops it?
- How or in what ways is it a problem?

How the situation constitutes a problem for a student, teacher, or parent may often be clear—but is it really? Consider ADHD. What does it mean? What does the client really want from intervention? How is the ADHD a problem? Is it a behavior problem, a grade problem, an attitude problem, and so on? In any case of uncertainty, which we believe is all the time, it is better for the practitioner to inquire about the "how," rather than assuming he or she really knows. *How* the situation constitutes a problem helps the practitioner understand the student, teacher, and parent's unique experience of the problem, identifies what intervention should address, and provides a key element to the client's theory of change. It often helps to assume a "slow to understand" stance to get the problem into concrete terms.

Consider Mark, a 16-year-old student who told the school counselor that he was depressed. When Mark was asked how his depression was a problem, he noted that it affected his ability to concentrate on homework and tests. Pursuing the "how" allows the practitioner to pinpoint the area where action may have the most effect. For example, if Mark is able to do something different about the concentration problem, it will very likely help his depression. The pursuit of specificity, then, helps define problems in such a way that allows more solution options.

Sometimes considering things in such a microscopic way leads to new understandings. People tend not to think of situations in such detail and become so familiar with the misery of the problem that they barely notice its mechanics. Dismantling the problem and examining its parts can lead to new insights. For example, consider Jamal, a high school senior who shared how he had been struggling with depression related to his dad's chronic drinking, and how he often was put in the middle of his parents' contentious divorce. After the practitioner asked him a series of questions on the specific details of how he "does" the depression and what the depression is about, Jamal ended the session with a surprising conclusion. He said that he knew what the counselor was driving at: If he were going to conquer his depression, he would have to stop bailing his dad out of trouble and deliver an ultimatum to his parents about staying out of their problems. And he did. Of course, the practitioner wasn't driving at anything. Sometimes taking the pieces of the puzzle apart provides just enough of a different perspective to get people going in a new direction.

PAT AND ANN REVISITED

Pat described the problem as Ann's depression, which was characterized by a general negative attitude, complaining, and boredom. Exploring how such behaviors constituted a problem revealed Pat's more personal struggles. When seen alone, Pat conveyed her helplessness. She described how she tried to comfort Ann, and went to great lengths to monitor the "depression" and help her daughter overcome it. Her real fear, she said, was that Ann's "early signs" would worsen, damning her to the bouts of depression that had plagued two previous generations of women in the family. Exploring how Ann's depression constituted a problem revealed that intervention should address Pat's strong desire to be helpful to her daughter.

When the practitioner saw Ann alone, she was quiet and sullen at first, but became animated and friendly when the conversation turned to the "mean" boys in her class. She insisted that she was not depressed, that her only problem was that the boys teased her, which, she said, happened to all the girls in her class. Ann denied that the boys might really like her, but her counselor remained skeptical. The delightful banter left no cause for concern.

Step 2: Exploring Solution Attempts

The next step is to contemplate what all the persons closely involved with the problem have been doing to resolve it. This may include family members, friends, fellow workers, professionals, and so on, depending on the circumstances. Again, this exploration focuses on actual behaviors, what people are doing and saying in their attempts to prevent a recurrence of the problem, or how they deal with it when it happens. Understanding solution attempts is the core of this approach. Interventions are designed from information about attempted solutions, and usually represent a shift in the opposite direction from the basic thrust of the unsuccessful attempts.

Pursuing solution attempts also offers an opportunity to explore solutions that have worked, even fleetingly. If a helpful past or current solution is discovered, the practitioner can capitalize on this success and build a solution based on this "exception" to the problem. This is precisely what happened in Mark's situation. While looking at his solutions, Mark identified an exception to his problem with concentration. He noted that when he studied with others, his concentration seemed better. Applying the solution-building format to Mark meant that he needed only to schedule more group study times and that he should organize his schoolwork around getting at least one other person to study with him. In each class, Mark quickly scoped out a study partner, joined any available study groups, and always attended any help sessions the teachers offered. Mark made studying with others a critical part of his school experience, and ultimately found that this was a very positive direction for him to follow.

Exploring solution attempts may also encourage students, parents, and teachers to consider avenues they haven't tried but were thinking about. Consider Erik, a 36-year-old single parent tormented by his 17-year-old's marijuana smoking. Erik tried a variety of things with Brent, including lectures, groundings, and education at a drug treatment center, but none had influenced Brent's marijuana use. When answering questions about solution attempts, Erik shared an idea he had been considering about requiring clean urine in exchange for driving privileges. In the ensuing discussion, Erik decided that Brent had pushed him around for too long and had made Erik feel guilty about the breakup of his marriage. Erik was encouraged to implement the idea, and the problem was resolved. New insights about problems can occur as a result of considering solutions in detail.

Discussing previous solutions enables the practitioner to avoid what has previously failed, amplify what has already worked, and permit the client's perceptions to remain central to the process. Questions regarding solution attempts include the following:

- What have you done about the problem?
- How did each of these things work or not work?
- What have other people done, or suggested doing, about the problem?
- What other things have you thought about trying?

Recall also that the discussion of prior solutions provides an excellent way to clarify the theories of change held by students, teachers, and parents. Inquiring about prior solutions allows the practitioner to hear the client's frank evaluation of previous attempts and appraisal of how change can occur.

PAT AND ANN REVISITED

Pat's solution attempts involved long discussions intended to comfort Ann. Pat also went to great lengths to prevent her daughter from being bored or sad. She invited Ann's friends over, invented games to play, and spent much of her time monitoring the "depression." Sometimes Pat took Ann shopping when she appeared sad. Pat's persistent attempts to help her daughter perpetuated and exacerbated the very problem they were intended to solve. Pat reported that none of her efforts were successful. She neither identified exceptions to the problem nor was enthusiastic about their discussion.

Exploring solution attempts also revealed more about Pat's theory of change. When asked about what others had suggested, Pat replied that everyone else, especially Ann's teacher, had attempted to persuade her that nothing was wrong, and that Ann was a normal 9-year-old. Of course these answers did not fit Pat's theory of change, and consequently were not effective. Exploring what others had suggested made it clear that Pat's genetic depression theory must be respected if intervention was to be successful.

Pat's criterion for success was explored and several goals were discussed. When asked to prioritize her goals, Pat identified seeing Ann smile more often, at least once a day, as a first sign of success. In addition, Pat said, "I need for you to verify what my psychiatrist has told me and what I already know in my heart, that Ann is depressed like me and my mother. I also want to know what to do to help my daughter!" Pat wanted to see Ann smile at least once a day, verification of her genetic theory, and suggestions about how she could help her daughter. Ann just wanted her mom to stop asking her whether she was depressed.

Step 3: Interrupting Solution Attempts

Here is where the strengths, resources, and ideas recruited from students, parents, and teachers come into play. All interventions must necessarily depend on the resources of clients. They are the ones that do the work of change and put into practice any ideas that emerge from collaborating with the school practitioner.

Recall how the very solutions people use to address a problem evolve into a vicious cycle: The more the problem occurs, the more attempted solutions are applied. Attempted solutions that fail to produce a desired change become the impetus for more of the problem. The MRI has taught us that despite the best of intentions, experience sometimes leads students, parents, teachers, and practitioners to continue holding on to a method even though the result is an intimate relationship with a brick wall.

Experience, then, can be a double-edged sword. For example, experience tells us that should we encounter a large, fast-moving, gray-colored animal, with thick pounding legs, big floppy ears, a long trunk, and tusks, emitting a loud trumpeting sound, we'd best move aside and let it pass because it is probably an elephant. Here experience has high predictive value. But when it comes to an unremitting problem, experience may not be as predictive and instead may lead to the same dead-end solutions.

Looking at the relationship between the problem and attempted solutions opens new options for consideration. Intervention ideas evolve from two questions: (1) What can the client do that will stop the current solution attempts? and (2) What other solutions can be suggested that run counter to those currently employed? Interventions can be broadly classified into two categories: *Do Something Else* and *Unleash the Client's Creativity*.

DO SOMETHING ELSE

Perhaps the simplest way to interrupt solution attempts is to encourage the client to alter the performance of the problem in some small but significant way. The task is simply to "do" the problem differently, to do something else. There are an unlimited number of ways to interrupt the problem cycle. Here are but a few that can be co-created with clients.

Observe the Problem. This strategy may be useful for any situation that is made worse by overattention and overintervention. This problem-busting idea simply suggests that students, parents, and teachers do absolutely nothing about the problem except observe it and record data about it. Observation tasks represent "something different" and often interrupt ineffective solution attempts, especially when people are pressing too hard. The idea is to stop the self-or-other harassment (which often takes place with the best of intentions) by performing a task that prevents the pressure for success. Sometimes taking the edge off, loosening the screws just a bit, is enough to allow a better outcome to occur or other interventions to take hold or be noticed.

Although observation tasks are useful for a broad range of problems, they may be particularly suitable for problems having to do with natural bodily functions. Sometimes, when these difficulties occur and people make willful, concerted efforts to fix them, they put themselves in a position of trying to coerce something that can only occur spontaneously. You cannot will yourself to sleep, or force yourself to be hungry. The trick here is to do something that interrupts the willful attempts that perpetuate the problem. For example, Jim, a junior struggling with an insomnia problem, tried a variety of strategies to "make himself" go to sleep. He read, took hot baths, and tried a variety of relaxation methods, but to no avail. The more he relentlessly tried to force himself to sleep, the more it seemed he stayed awake. The counselor suggested that Jim observe his sleeping problem. For Jim, this meant observing his sleeping problem for a week, recording the time he goes to bed, noting how long it takes him to fall asleep, and noting his thoughts while lying in bed. Jim made it until the third night, when his natural sleeping rhythm returned. Observation tasks often free the individual up to let nature take its course without the client's well-meaning interference. Chapter 6 presents an example of this idea with parents whose well-intended efforts are compounding their child's school avoidance problem.

Invite What You Dread. This strategy may be useful for any situation in which students, parents, or teachers seem to be trying to solve the problem by avoiding it. It is perhaps especially helpful for those struggling with recurring negative feelings or unwanted thoughts. These individuals often believe that they will be swept away by the feelings or thoughts if they allow them to occur: that once the floodgates are opened, they will lose total control and drown. They spend a considerable amount of energy holding down the fort—attempting to ward off the feelings or thoughts or to stop them when they appear. Unfortunately, despite their constant vigilance, they find that the unwanted feelings or thoughts are always lurking, ready to strike at the most inopportune moments. There is always a breach in the wall. In many ways, the intrusive thoughts and feelings are made all the more powerful by all the effort to prevent or avoid their occurrence. What is useful here is to expose the struggling person to the avoided situation, thoughts, or emotions in a way that perfect mastery or success is not an expectation; that is, to allow the person to experience the troubling circumstance, learn from it, and move on with life.

A useful way to control negative feelings and intrusive thoughts is to make them happen, but in a way that provides a little distance. When we are troubled by unwanted thoughts or feelings, they seem to be completely outside of our control. They hit us out of the blue, which only makes us continually look up, like Chicken Little, awaiting the fall of more of the sky. "Invite What You Dread" makes a dramatic shift by making an involuntary action voluntary. Something that has been perceived as out of the individual's control is now under his or her control. This process makes the client the master instead of the servant of feelings or thoughts. Rather than opening Pandora's Box, many find that giving the thoughts or feelings concerted airtime reduces them over time, allowing them to fade into the background.

For example, Sandra, a sophomore, reported to the school practitioner that she felt so depressed that she went to bed as soon as she got home from school. This was such a paradox to her because her life was going so well! Sandra had just moved and found the new school and the exciting new city to be what she always wanted. It should have made her happy. Instead, Sandra wound up incessantly trying to convince herself to be happy while simultaneously avoiding all that was negative about her circumstance. This only resulted in more and more feelings of hopelessness and more and more sleep. She examined her problem cycle with the school counselor, the problem of her depression (specifically, sleeping too much) and her solutions (primarily avoiding any feeling of depression because she shouldn't feel that way). The practitioner suggested "Invite What You Dread," that Sandra set time aside each day when she arrived home from school to give the depression its due. Sandra was asked to think of her move, the new city, and how much she missed her friends. She started to cry and instead of quickly drying her tears, she let it go. Sandra did this every day and found that the intensity of the feelings diminished and her tears slowed down. As this occurred, she felt more energetic and slept less. Chapter 6 presents an example of

"Invite What You Dread" with a child struggling with unwanted thoughts about a teacher.

Go with the Flow. This group of strategies covers about any dispute or disagreement in which one person is trying to get another person to do something that he or she is not so motivated to do, or where one person sees a problem and the other doesn't (like Pat and Ann). It starts with simply trying to bring the problem to the other person's attention, and then escalates to *really* bringing the problem to the other's attention by confronting, persuading, reasoning, or arguing. Go with the flow fits many relational conflicts because people often respond to any mention of a problem or request for change with natural defensiveness, perhaps especially adolescents. This pressure to change may prevent the other person from considering the alternatives and possibly changing the problem on his or her own. This method makes it clear that the direct pressure is off.

Go with the flow requires the one desiring the change to accept and even encourage the other person's actions, thereby avoiding a contrary position. This strategy can take as many different forms as there are situations. By virtue of encouraging things to stay the same, the context in which the problem occurs is dramatically changed. Consider Cheryl, a freshman English teacher who consulted the practitioner because of the incessant criticism of one of her students. Tim always found something wrong with Cheryl's class and unfailingly reported every perceived shortcoming to Cheryl. At first Cheryl accepted the criticisms in a good-natured way, but now they were really getting on her nerves. The situation degenerated into a cycle of criticism with Cheryl defending her actions to Tim, followed by further criticisms of her inability to take feedback, and so on.

Consider how go with the flow could be useful in this situation. One could simply find something about the criticism to agree with or could ask the person for feedback before he or she had an opportunity to criticize. These options were discussed with Cheryl, but she chose another variation called "agree and exaggerate" (Duncan & Rock, 2005) because she liked the way it turned the tables on Tim. This version of go with the flow suggests that the criticized individual agree with the criticisms and even expand or exaggerate them: "Yes, I'm a terrible lecturer, and I can't believe you're hearty enough to stay awake the entire period;" "Not only are my tests lousy, but I'm coming to believe that I am generally a rotten teacher. I'm amazed you continue to put up with me." The idea is to agree with the words, but not in any way change behavior. It is very important not to sound sarcastic. That just creates hostility.

Consider the logic presented to Cheryl: If you agree and the criticizer accepts it, you still do whatever you want, the argument is over, and you didn't get angry and defensive. So, you win. If he or she disagrees with you (remember, you are now accepting criticism), that means he or she is absolving you of blame. So you still win. Cheryl liked the logic, especially the part about not feeling so defensive. She tried it with Tim, who after a few occurrences and few puzzled looks (but no further discussion), said, "No, I didn't mean it that way. I think you're a great teacher." Go with the flow is also illustrated with Pat and Ann later in this chapter.

All categories of interrupting the problem cycle share a very important commonality, that is, the theme of doing something noticeably different when students, teachers, and parents are faced with situations in which they feel stuck. Interrupting business as usual creates possibilities for rapid change.

"Do Something Else" requires only that school practitioners collaborate with clients to experiment with the problem cycle. It can take as many forms as there are people. For example, 15-year-old Matt was frustrated because he could not urinate in school restrooms—the longer he stood there without going, the more he anxious be became. He felt hopeless and demoralized. Matt had tried a variety of relaxation and self-talk strategies, but the problem and its discomfort persisted. Matt and the school practitioner brainstormed ways that he could change the "doing" of the problem, and Matt intimated that he was beginning to feel angry about the whole thing. Subsequently, the practitioner suggested that instead of responding with hopelessness when the problem occurred, that Matt work himself up to a good anger—about how this problem interfered with his comfort and added a big hassle to his life. Matt allowed himself, when standing in front of the urinal, to become incensed—downright pissed off. And he started to go. Changing the feeling from passive resignation to anger paid off. Doing something else allows different possibilities.

UNLEASH THE CLIENT'S CREATIVITY

Another option to interrupt client solution attempts is to encourage the client to let go of inhibitions and release his or her natural creativity.

The school practitioner (1) acknowledges that "something different" is required, and that it is unclear exactly what that could be at the time, and (2) encourages the student, parent, or teacher to "Try Something Different" in response to the problem during the next week. We are continually amazed by the ingenuity and resourcefulness of clients when given this task.

For example, a couple saw the school counselor because they were extremely upset about their 13-year-old son's intimidating temper tantrums and power plays. He became so loud, angry, and disruptive, they thought of him as the Incredible Hulk. The family had been through therapy and had tried many conventional methods to no avail.

In an attempt to stop their current solution attempts, the school counselor asked the couple to unleash their creativity and try something else that flew in the face of all the traditional methods that had failed. When they came back, they laughingly reported what they had done during the last Incredible Hulk episode. Right when he started to rant, the couple quietly stood up, went into their bedroom and locked the door. They began making squealing, grunting, and groaning noises. The tantrums stopped.

Why? Because of the relationship between the problem and the applied solutions. The parents changed the way they approached the problem (endless talk, pleading, punishments) and enabled a different response from their son. Many times, a small adjustment is all that is needed for some much-needed relief. Recall that the only task is to change how clients "do" the problem—to change something, almost anything, when the problem occurs. Changing the doing can be as outrageous as the grunting and groaning parents or it can be very subtle. The idea is to encourage clients to unleash their creativity and experiment, knowing that when the current solutions are changed, the problem will be as well. For example, instead of her usual angry tirade when her son Wade came home late at night, Susan greeted her apprehensive son with a long, passionate discussion about the war in Iraq, and intimated how much she enjoyed such discussions. Wade started coming home on time more often.

After an intervention is suggested, the school practitioner follows up with students, parents, and teachers to review the results of their experiment with doing the problem differently. If improvement is noted, the task becomes to expand and empower the change as was discussed previously.

Problem Busting with Pat and Ann

Detailing the Problem. Who?: Ann. *What?*: Genetic depression, negative attitude, and sadness. *To whom is it a problem?*: Pat. *How is it a problem?*: Pat feels helpless.

Exploring Solution Attempts. (1) Lecturing, (2) cheerleading, (3) monitoring, (4) trying to fix or help (e.g., calling friends, shopping), and (5) others' solutions, revolving around suggesting that nothing was wrong.

Client's Goals. To observe Ann smiling more. Other goals included verification of the genetic depression theory and suggestions about how to help Ann.

Client's Theory of Change. Ann was genetically disposed to depression, just like Pat and her mother; honoring Pat's theory required the practitioner to select interventions that would interrupt solution attempts while respecting Pat's genetic perspective of depression.

Interrupting Solution Attempts by Doing Something Else. (1) What can Pat do that will stop the current solution attempts? (2) What other solutions can be suggested that run counter to the solutions currently employed? Using a popular view of genetic influences on behavior (the diathesis-stress paradigm) to fit Pat's theory, the practitioner suggested that, given the familial predisposition to depression, environmental interventions were critical. Perhaps Pat could assist Ann in (1) "coping with" the depression rather than fixing it, and (2) accepting and encouraging it rather than stopping it (Invite What You Dread).

The school practitioner accepted Pat's genetic depression theory, validated her worry as appropriate given the family history, and noted her obvious love and concern for her daughter. A story of competent parenthood and love competed with the story of a "certifiable nut" and "loose cannon." Surprised and relieved, Pat said, "Oh, you see it, too." She relaxed and was ready to shift the conversation to what might help in the present situation. Validation of a client's viewpoint, even when others disagree, often opens the conversation to new ideas and directions.

Staying with the genetic perspective, the practitioner suggested that while there was a strong familial predisposition to depression, the key to whether the depression actually appeared was what happened in Ann's environment. The practitioner proposed that perhaps Pat could help Ann by helping her deal with her depression.

SP: You may be able to help Ann cope with her depression by validating her concerns, boredom, and sadness when she expresses it—and then allowing her the space to sort it out herself. For example, if Ann says, "I'm bored, there's nothing to do around here; I hate it when no one is around to play with," what I am suggesting that you say in return is "Yes, it must be tough to be all alone in the house with nobody to play with." By validating her concern, she will feel understood, and the ball will essentially be back in her court to deal with the boredom. The hard part for parents is to resist the temptation to cheer up, entertain, or otherwise coerce the kid to feel better. Parents sometimes discount a child's negative feelings out of love. No one wants their kids to experience anything negative. Is this making any sense?

PAT: Yes it is, because I'm a stroker, I'm always upbeat and positive with her . . . always telling her how smart and pretty she is and how school is fun. I guess I sort of discount her feelings and it's not helping. Is that what you are getting at? (*All ears, she encourages the practitioner to continue.*)

SP: Exactly, except you are not doing anything wrong. What I am suggesting is that you "lean to" her depression, invite its expression, and enable Ann to develop coping strategies. Another way of looking at this is to, in general, respond to "gloom and doom" comments with agreement and even with a slight exaggeration of her original complaint. For example, to the comment, "I hate school," you may respond, "School can certainly be a bummer, and the worst of it is there's so much more to go." In essence, you are teaching her how to cope with it by allowing her some time and space to deal with it.

PAT: I guess you just don't expect kids to have bad feelings and you want to protect them from any hurt. But that's impossible to do. They suffer just as we do. Yeah, I need to allow her to be and support her feelings, even if it's negative. When you say exaggeration, I'm thinking that particularly to her critical comments about herself, how about if I exaggerate them to the point of ridiculousness?

Like if she says she's ugly, I'll say, "Yeah, you're so ugly I've had to replace three broken mirrors because you looked in them," instead of trying to convince her how pretty she is.

SP: Sounds great!

The practitioner intervened by suggesting that Pat help Ann work through and learn to cope with her depression. Pat could facilitate the process by encouraging expression of Ann's concerns, validating them, and even exaggerating them, rather than reacting against them. Pat responded very positively to the suggestions and immediately began discussing their application, a good sign of a good fit with her theory of change.

Intervention was designed to interrupt and reverse Pat's solution attempts. The teacher and principal had already attempted to convince Pat that Ann was a normal 9-year-old, but Pat did not believe it and therefore did not respond to suggestions that Ann could be left to her own devices. After it became clear that the practitioner was not going to challenge her beliefs, Pat showed greater flexibility and softened her viewpoint about Ann's genetic depression. The "agree and exaggerate" intervention interrupted Pat's solution attempts of cheering and reassuring Ann, while honoring Pat's theory of genetic depression.

Pat altered the proposed suggestions to fit her sense of humor and strengths, so her exaggerations of Ann's complaints were funny instead of the serious fare the school practitioner had suggested. Pat applied her personalized adaptations of the suggestions and returned for two more meetings. She reported that Ann was smiling more and complaining less. Pat concluded that her daughter was only mildly predisposed to depression and was satisfied that an antidepressant was not needed.

THE BOTTOM LINE OF PROBLEM BUSTING

Using the strengths, experiences, and ideas of students, parents, and teachers, the Three-Step Problem-Busting Interview encourages clients to break the law of "if at first you don't succeed, try, try, again." It seeks to identify the problem–solution cycle and then unleash both the school practitioner's and client's creativity to break it. There are countless ways to do something different and interrupt solutions that are not working. Remember that *what* is done is not as important as actually doing something different. Feel free to experiment! Discuss the options that strike a chord with students, parents, and teachers and collaborate on strategies that fit with their sensibilities about change.

CONCLUSIONS

The chapter described how to enlist student, parent, and teacher resources and ideas—to recruit the heroic client—and offered two interview formats that harvest change possibilities. Openness to the rich field of opportunities for rapid change is the ideal characterization of the successful practitioner. The interview methods of *solution building* and *problem busting* are conceptually simple and pragmatic: Either find something that works and encourage people to do more of it, or interrupt solution attempts and encourage people to try something else. However, application of the methods can be challenging because it requires a shift in the way we often approach school problems and the people who experience them. Instead of attempting to resolve problems by focusing mainly on what is wrong with clients, both interviewing formats build upon what is right about people and their circumstances.

Despite the advantages of the methods and ideas we have described, it is not enough. Yes, at first blush, tapping into client resources, ensuring the client's positive experience of the alliance, and accommodating intervention to the client's theory of change capitalizes on the two largest contributors to success. At the same time, there is a danger—any concrete application across clients merely leads to the creation of another model. On this point, the research is clear: Models ultimately matter little in terms of outcome.

To remedy the mere creation of yet another model and to give clients the voice in intervention that the research literature says they deserve, we routinely solicit client feedback about the services they receive. We have learned that to be brief and effective is to be outcome informed. Chapter 4 takes "The Client Knows Best" guideline to a new level, demonstrating a remarkably easy way to improve effectiveness while legitimizing school-based services.

CHAPTER 4

♦ ♦ ♦

Assessment 2
Becoming Outcome Informed

♦

The proof of the pudding is in the eating.
—MIGUEL DE CERVANTES

In what has become one of the most cited articles in the business literature, Levitt (1975) shows how various industries, from the railroads to Hollywood, suffered dramatic reversals in fortune when they became "product-oriented instead of customer-oriented"(p. 19). Movie moguls, for instance, were caught totally off guard by the television industry because they wrongly thought themselves in the movie rather than entertainment business. As famed director and studio executive, Darryl F. Zanuck, boldly asserted, "Television won't be able to hold onto any market it captures after the first six months. People will soon get tired of staring at a plywood box every night" (Lee, 2000). Such extraordinary lack of foresight eventually forced the closure of once powerful studios and bankrupted numerous high rollers in the trade.

Similarly, school practice has traditionally acted as though it were in the intervention business rather than the business of change. The field's focus on the means of producing change (i.e., models, techniques, intervention process) has been and continues to be on the wrong track.

The important question is not what constitutes effective intervention, but whether students, parents, and teachers experience the changes they desire.

In this second of two chapters devoted to assessment, we suggest that practitioners can avoid the fate of a "product orientation" by becoming outcome informed. Being outcome informed means measuring the effectiveness and fit of services from the vantage point of students, parents, and teachers, and using the collected information as a guide to enhance what's working and modify or quit whatever is not working. Chapter 4 combines our three principles of intervention—"The Client Knows Best," "Reliance on the Alliance," and "If First You Don't Succeed, Try Something Different"—and lays out the details of becoming outcome informed. This chapter advocates for the formal inclusion of client voices, providing enough foundation for you to begin an outcome project at your school. We argue that assessing outcome not only improves the effectiveness of intervention, but also provides school practitioners with a method of legitimizing their services.

CHANGE IS PREDICTABLE

We all know that no practitioner is effective with everyone; in fact, if school practitioners are like mental health professionals, their effectiveness likely ranges from 20 to 70% (Hansen & Lambert, 2003). Until now, however, little has been done to find who is not benefiting so that something different could occur. This is unfortunate because *the general trajectory of change in successful intervention is highly predictable*, with most change occurring earlier rather than later (Brown, Dreis, & Nace, 1999; Haas, Hill, Lambert, & Morrell, 2002; Howard, Moras, Brill, Martinovich, & Lutz, 1996; Whipple et al., 2003). Recall the Cannabis Youth Treatment study mentioned in Chapter 2. Although contact continued with the youth and families in this study for a year, the lion's share of change in those youth who responded favorably to intervention happened in the first 3 months. Change, if it is going to occur, tends to start early.

In fact, the client's subjective experience of meaningful change in the first few meetings predicts whether a given pairing of client and practitioner will result in a successful outcome (Haas et al., 2002; Lambert et al., 2001). Brown et al. (1999) found that relationships in which no improvement occurred by the third visit did not on average result in improvement over the entire course of intervention. This study further showed that clients who worsened by the third meeting were twice as likely to drop out than those who reported progress. Importantly, variables such as diagnosis, severity, family support, and type of intervention were "*not* . . . as important [in predicting eventual outcome] as knowing whether or not the treatment being provided [was] actually working" (p. 404, emphasis added).

Early progress, then, has emerged as a robust predictor of ultimate outcome. This finding dovetails with another potent predictor identified in Chapter 2—namely, the client's early ratings of the alliance. The conclusion to be drawn: School practitioners do not need to know ahead of time what approach to use for a given diagnosis or problem as much as whether the current relationship is a good fit and providing benefit, and, if not, be able to adjust early enough to maximize the chances of success. Taking advantage of these two potent predictors of outcome requires taking "The Client Knows Best" literally, and "Trying Something Different" when client feedback reveals no change.

TRACKING OUTCOME AND ALLIANCE

A variety of approaches exist for evaluating the outcome of intervention. Most efforts draw on well-established measures designed mainly for research purposes, both practitioner- and client-rated, as well as observer ratings, physiological indices, and environmental information (Lambert, Ogles, & Masters, 1992). Although these multidimensional assessments of outcome are valid and reliable, their complexity, length of administration, scoring, and interpretation often render them infeasible for many settings. In truth, the average practitioner in today's schools is overloaded with paperwork and other activities not related to service (e.g., phone calls, team meetings, individualized service plans, assessments, etc.). Clearly, this reality must be considered when becoming outcome informed. Brown et al. (1999), for example, found that the majority of practitioners did not consider practical any measure or combination of measures that took more than 5 minutes to complete, score, and interpret. As a result, a strong argument can be made for adopting measures that are brief in addition to being reliable and valid.

To encourage the collaborative discussion of outcome with clients,

Miller and Duncan (2000) developed the Outcome Rating Scale (ORS) as a brief alternative to longer measures. The ORS assesses three dimensions of client functioning: (1) personal or symptomatic distress (measuring individual well-being), (2) interpersonal well-being (measuring how well the client is getting along in intimate relationships), and (3) social role (measuring satisfaction with work/school and relationships outside of the home). Changes in these three areas are widely considered to be valid indicators of successful outcome (Lambert et al., 1996).

The ORS simply translates these three areas and an overall rating into a visual analogue format of four 10-centimeter lines, with instructions to place a mark on each line with low estimates to the left and high to the right (see Appendix B). The four 10-centimeter lines add to a total score of 40. The score is simply the summation of the marks made by the client to the nearest millimeter on each of the four lines, measured by a centimeter ruler or available template. A score of 25, the clinical cutoff, differentiates those who are experiencing enough distress to be in a helping relationship from those who are not. Those scoring above 25 typically reflect scores of persons not receiving services. For adolescents, the cutoff score is 28, and for children under 12 the cutoff is 33 (Duncan, Sparks, Miller, Bohanske, & Claud, in press).

In addition to brevity and ease of administration, visual analogue scales enjoy high face validity with clients, something typically missing from more technical measures that seem distant from the client's experience. Because of the ORS's simplicity, feedback is immediately available for use *at the time the service is delivered.* Any delay necessarily limits the usefulness of the results.

The ORS rates at a seventh-grade reading level, making it feasible for most adults and adolescents who seek or are referred for intervention. Students, parents, and teachers have little difficulty connecting their day-to-day lived experience to the ORS and translating it into the specifics of their circumstances. As for practitioners, Miller, Duncan, Brown, Sparks, and Claud (2003) reported that counselors found the measure far easier to use and integrate into everyday practice than they did longer outcome measures. The Child ORS (CORS) (Duncan, Miller, & Sparks, 2003a; see Appendix B), for children 12 and under, is similar in format but contains child-friendly language as well as smiley and frowny faces to aid the child's understanding. Parents and teachers use the ORS to rate students over 12 and the CORS for children 12 and under. The ORS and CORS are free for individual use and may be downloaded in many languages from *www.talkingcure.com.*

The Session Rating Scale: Monitoring Fit

Even though it adds more precious time to the outcome management process, partnering with the client to monitor the fit of the service with the client's expectations about the relationship and change is important. The addition of an ongoing assessment of the alliance enables practitioners to identify and correct areas of weakness in the delivery of services before these weaknesses exert a negative effect on outcome.

Recall that clients' ratings of the alliance are more predictive of improvement than the type of intervention or the practitioner's ratings of the alliance. Recognizing these consistent findings, Johnson (1995) created the Session Rating Scale (SRS) to help track his own progress with clients. Miller, Duncan, and Johnson (2001) later modified the SRS to be a briefer alternative to longer research-based alliance measures, in order to encourage routine conversations with clients about the alliance. A visual analogue scale, the SRS contains four items. First, a relationship scale rates the meeting on a continuum from "I did not feel heard, understood, and respected" to "I felt heard, understood, and respected." Second is a goals and topics scale that rates the conversation on a continuum from "We did not work on or talk about what I wanted to work on or talk about" to "We worked on or talked about what I wanted to work on or talk about." Third is an approach or method scale (an indication of a match with the client's theory of change) requiring the client to rate the meeting on a continuum from "The approach is not a good fit for me" to "The approach is a good fit for me." Finally, the fourth scale looks at how the client perceives the encounter in total along the continuum "There was something missing in the session today" to "Overall, today's session was right for me."

The SRS simply translates what is known about the alliance into four visual analogue scales, with instructions to place a mark on a line with negative responses depicted on the left and positive responses indicated on the right. The SRS allows alliance feedback in real time so that problems may be addressed. In addition to assessing factors that research has linked to positive outcomes, the SRS is highly feasible (high likelihood of use—see next section of this chapter). Like the ORS, the instrument takes less than a minute to administer and score. Furthermore, the content of the items makes sense to both clients and practitioners, giving the scale good face validity. The SRS is scored similarly to the ORS, by adding the total of the client's marks on the four 10-centimeter lines. The total score falls into three categories:

- SRS score between 0 and 34 reflects a poor alliance.
- SRS score between 35 and 38 reflects a fair alliance.
- SRS score between 39 and 40 reflects a good alliance.

The SRS is also applicable with adolescents, and a child version, the Child Session Rating Scale (CSRS) for children under 12 is also available (Duncan, Miller, & Sparks, 2003b). Remarkably, the CSRS is the first alliance scale for children under 12. The SRS and CSRS are free for individual use and may be downloaded in many languages from *www. talkingcure.com.*

Using the ORS and SRS in concert tracks both outcome *and* the alliance, thereby taking advantage of the two known predictors of outcome. This outcome management process partners with students, parents, and teachers to address the effectiveness, fit, and accountability of services. The practitioner uses the measures in collaboration with clients to amplify their voices during the intervention process, finally inviting clients into the inner circle.

Reliability, Validity, and Feasibility of the ORS and SRS

The ORS/CORS and SRS/CSRS have demonstrated their reliability and validity (Duncan, Miller, Sparks, Claud, et al., 2003; Miller et al., 2003; Duncan et al., in press), and perhaps more importantly, their *feasibility.* Feasibility involves the likelihood that the instrument will be used; feasibility is the degree to which an instrument can be explained, completed, and interpreted quickly and easily. If outcome measures do not meet the time demands of actual school practice, practitioners and clients alike may meet them with reluctance at best, and resistance at worst.

Miller et al. (2003) examined utilization rates over time in two sites with similar clients and mandates to assess the feasibility of the ORS as compared to a longer outcome measure, The Outcome Questionnaire 45.2 (OQ). The overall utilization rate after 1 year was 25% for the OQ and 89% for the ORS. Similarly, Duncan, Miller, Sparks, Claud, et al. (2003) examined compliance rates among practitioners at similar agencies; one agency implemented the SRS and the other used the 12-item Working Alliance Inventory (WAI) (Horvath & Greenberg, 1989). After 1 year, the SRS enjoyed a 96% utilization rate while the WAI was used only 29% of the time. Gains in feasibility offset losses in reliability and validity when switching to shorter measures like the ORS and SRS.

Obviously, no matter how reliable and valid a measure is, if it is not used, the benefits of outcome management will not be realized.

The ORS/CORS and SRS/CSRS in Action

Providing feedback to practitioners regarding clients' experience of the alliance and progress via the SRS and ORS has been shown to result in significant improvements in both client retention and outcome. For example, Miller, Duncan, Brown, Sorrell, and Chalk (2006) found that clients of practitioners who opted out of completing the SRS were twice as likely to drop out and three to four times more likely to have a negative outcome. In the same study, the average effect size of services at the agency where both measures were employed shifted from 0.39 to 0.79—doubling the effectiveness of this agency in a sample of 6,224 clients.

As incredible as the results may appear, they are consistent with findings from other researchers. In a meta-analysis of three studies, Lambert et al. (2003) reported that those helping relationships at risk for a negative outcome which received formal feedback were, at the conclusion of intervention, better off than 65% of those without information regarding progress. In another study, Whipple et al. (2003) found that clients whose practitioners had access to outcome *and* alliance information were less likely to deteriorate, more likely to stay longer, and *twice as likely* to achieve a significant change.

Notably, these results were obtained without any attempt to organize, systematize, or otherwise control intervention process. Neither were the practitioners in these studies trained in any new modalities, techniques, or diagnostic procedures. Rather, they were completely free to engage their clients in the manner they saw fit. Availability of formal client feedback was the only constant in an otherwise diverse intervention environment.

Client feedback on the ORS/CORS about the success or failure of intervention can provide valuable information about the match between client, practitioner, and approach. In particular, such feedback informs key decisions about how to tailor intervention to the specific needs and characteristics of individual clients and when to terminate or refer to another practitioner or venue of service when the client is not benefiting. Regarding the alliance, since research indicates that clients frequently drop out *before* discussing problems in the alliance, the SRS provides the opportunity to remedy whatever problems exist. The benefits described here, when taken in combination with the field's obvious failure to discover and systematize intervention process in a manner that reliably improves success, have led us to conclude that the best hope for the field will be found in outcome management.

PARTNERING WITH STUDENTS, PARENTS, AND TEACHERS: THE NUTS AND BOLTS

All scoring and interpretation of the measures are done together *with* clients. This not only represents a radical departure from traditional assessment but also gives students, parents, and teachers a new way to look at and comment on their experience of both progress and the fit of intervention. Assessment, rather than an expert-driven evaluation of the client, becomes a pivotal part of the relationship and change itself (Duncan et al., 2004).

Partnering with students, parents, and teachers to monitor outcome and fit actually starts before formal intervention, for both practitioners and clients. Practitioners have to think that privileging the client's perceptions, ideas, and experiences is a good thing. If the school professional does not value the client's perspective and does not believe that the client should be an active participants in the decisions that affect him or her, the proposed outcome process will have little impact. Clients also need to be on board. This means informing students, parents, and teachers about the nature of the partnership when scheduling the first contact and creating a feedback culture in which their voice is essential. For example, the practitioner could say:

> "[to an older student, parent, or teacher] I want to help you reach your goals. I have found it important to monitor progress from meeting to meeting using two very short paper-and-pencil forms. Your ongoing feedback will tell us if we are on track, need to change something about our approach, or need to include other resources or referrals to help you get what you want. Is that something you think you can help me with?"

> "[to a younger student] I really want things to get better for you here at school. To help me do that, I like to get students to

fill out two little forms that will tell us if we are getting some-where. They are kind of fun, and are a way of making sure I don't forget about your ideas. Can you help me out with this?"

In a typical school setting, the practitioner would give the student, parent, or teacher the ORS (or CORS) *prior* to each meeting and the SRS (or CSRS) toward the end. With regard to the ORS, it is useful, if possi-ble, to have the instrument available *prior* to the meeting. Many clients will complete the ORS (some will even plot their scores on provided graphs) and greet the practitioner already discussing the implications. Using a scale that is simple enough for students and adults to score and interpret not only speeds the process but also increases client engage-ment in the evaluation of the services. Anything that increases participa-tion is likely to have a beneficial impact on outcome.

Step 1: Introducing the ORS in the First Meeting

Establishing a feedback culture in which the client's voice is privileged has already begun in the first scheduling contact. In the first meeting, that culture is continued. It is important to avoid technical jargon, and instead explain the purpose of the measures and their rationale in a nat-ural, commonsense way. The overwhelming majority of people think monitoring outcome is a great idea. The main point here is to make the monitoring part of a relaxed and ordinary way of having conversations and working. The specific words are not important. The practitioner's interest in the client's desired outcome speaks volumes about his or her commitment to the individual and the quality of service (Duncan & Sparks, 2002).

"[to an older student, parent, or teacher] Remember our earlier conversation? During the course of our work together, I will be giving you two very short forms asking you how you think things are going and whether you think things are on track. To make the most of our time together and get the best outcome, it is important to make sure we are on the same page with one another about how you are doing, how we are doing, and where we are going. We will be using your answers to keep us on track. Will that be okay with you?"

"[to a younger student] Here is that paper with smiley and frowny faces I mentioned to you. This funny form allows me to track where you're at, how you're doing, how things are changing, or if they are not changing. It allows us to know whether I am being helpful. It only takes a minute to do and most students find it to be very helpful. Would you like to give it a try? Great!"

Step 2: Incorporating the ORS in the First Meeting

Using the measures with the involved adults and the student of concern allows multiple perspectives to be both acknowledged and utilized. The measures encourage conversations about similarities and differences of individual ratings, and they allow practitioners to attend to each person's perspective of both change and the alliance. They provide a common ground on which to make comparisons and draw distinctions, allowing each individual to be part of the discussion of what needs to happen next. It is not unusual for students to hold different perspectives than their teachers and parents. Using a graph with different-colored lines for each person helps illustrate varying viewpoints and can open up a productive conversation. The CSRS and SRS give practitioners a chance to see which, if any, participants in intervention are feeling the least connected. The practitioner then has accurate knowledge of where to focus more attention.

The ORS/CORS pinpoints where the client is and allows a comparison point for later sessions. Incorporating the ORS entails simply bringing the student, parent, or teacher's initial and subsequent results into the conversation for discussion, clarification, and problem solving.

"[to a student] From your ORS it looks like you're experiencing some real problems. [Or:] From your score, it looks like you're feeling okay. What brings you here today? [Or:] Your total score is 15—wow, that's pretty low. A score under 28 indicates people who are in enough distress to seek help. Things must be pretty tough for you. What's going on?

"The way this ORS works is that marks toward the left (or scores under 25) indicate that things are hard for you now or you are hurting enough to bring you to see me. Your score on the individual scale indicates that you are really having a hard time. Would you like to tell me about it? [Or if all the marks are to the right:] Generally when people make their marks so far to the right (or when people score above 25 [or 28 or 33]), it is an indication that things are going well for them. What is it that brought you here now?"

"[to a teacher] Your rating of this student reflects that you are quite concerned about her, especially in school and personal well-being. Does this make sense with what you are thinking? [Or:] Your rating on the CORS is 34, which indicates that this child is doing very well overall, but that you have some concern with the student's school performance or behavior. Is that accurate?"

Because the ORS has face validity, clients regularly remark about their score on the different scales in relation to the reason they are seeking intervention. In other situations the practitioner must initiate the connection between the client's descriptions of the reasons for services and the client's scores on the ORS. The ORS makes no sense unless it is connected to the described experience of the student, parent, or teacher's life. This is a critical point because both the practitioner and the client must know what the mark on the line represents to the client and what will need to happen so that the client will both realize a change *and* indicate that change on the ORS. The line on the ORS is irrelevant until and unless the client bestows meaning on it.

At some point in the meeting, the practitioner needs only to pick up on the client's comments and connect them to the ORS:

"[to a student] Oh, okay, it sounds like dealing with the loss of your brother [or relationship with your teacher, sister's drinking, or anxiety attacks, etc.] is an important part of what we are doing here. Does the distress from that situation account for your mark here on the Individual [or other] scale on the ORS? Okay, so what do you think will need to happen for that mark to move toward the right?"

"[to a teacher] Okay, so the talking out in class and then talking back to you when you correct him are your main concerns? And are those the situations that account for your mark on the school scale? Okay, what do you think you would notice if your mark moved one centimeter to the right?"

The ORS, by design, is a general outcome instrument and provides no specific content to direct client or practitioner impressions. The ORS offers only a bare skeleton to which clients must add the flesh and blood of their experiences, into which they breathe life with their ideas and perceptions. At the moment in which students, parents, and teachers connect the marks on the ORS with the situations that are distressing, the ORS becomes a meaningful measure of their progress.

Revisiting Sean, Nicole, and Ms. White; Pat and Ann; Beth and Jermaine

Consider the use of the instruments with clients introduced in Chapter 3. Recall Sean and his difficulties in the classroom and with bed-wetting. Sean rated himself a 28.1 on the CORS; Nicole (Mom) rated Sean a 20.3 and Ms. White (teacher) rated him a 23.6. Each person's concerns were connected to the marks they made on the different scales. Sean's bed-wetting problem was connected to his mark (a 7.2) on the individual line; Nicole's perspective of Sean's difficulties was connected to both the personal well-being scale and the school scale (she scored Sean a 6.4 on the individual and 6 on the school scale); and Ms. White's description of Sean's difficulties in the classroom was connected to her rating of Sean (5.1) on the school scale. These connections, of those squiggly marks on the measures to each person's described experience of his or her life, led to a useful conversation about what it would take to move the marks just 1 centimeter to the right.

Recall Pat and her view that her 9-year-old daughter Ann was genetically depressed, despite the protestations of everyone in contact with Ann. Pat's rating of Ann on the CORS was 16.6, while Ann rated herself a 35.4. It is not unusual for students to rate themselves much higher than teachers or parents because students are often "involuntary" clients who are talking to practitioners because of someone else's concerns. Remember that Pat saw a serious problem, while Ann saw the only problem, besides mean boys, as being her mother. Their ratings reflected these perspectives.

Finally, recall Jermaine's problems with screaming in the classroom and not completing required work. The teacher, Beth, rated Jermaine a

12 on the CORS, reflecting her perspective of how troubled she believed Jermaine to be in several life domains. Given that the school practitioner only worked with Beth, and Jermaine was receiving services from another counselor, Jermaine's ratings of himself were not obtained.

Step 3: Introducing the SRS

The SRS, like the ORS, is best presented in a relaxed way that is seamlessly integrated into the practitioner's typical way of working. The use of the SRS continues the culture of client privilege and feedback, and opens space for the student, parent, or teacher's voice about the alliance. The SRS or CSRS is given at the end of the meeting, leaving enough time for discussing the client's responses.

> "[to a parent, teacher, or older student] Let's take a minute and have you fill out the other form that asks your opinion about our work together. It's kind of like taking the temperature of our relationship today. Are we too hot or too cold? This information helps me stay on track. The ultimate purpose of using these forms is to make every possible effort to make our work together beneficial. Would that be okay with you?"

> "[to a younger student] Before we wrap up I would like to ask you to fill out another one of those forms that has faces on it. This one deals with how you think I am doing. That's right— you get to grade me! It is very important to me to make sure that this is going well for you. Can you help me out?"

Step 4: Incorporating the SRS

Because the SRS/CSRS is easy to score and interpret, the practitioner can do a quick visual check and integrate it into the conversation. If the SRS looks good (each mark is placed at least 9 centimeters from the left), the practitioner need only comment on that fact and invite any other comments or suggestions. If the client has marked any scales lower than 9 centimeters, the practitioner should follow up. Clients tend to score all alliance measures highly, so the practitioner should address any hints of a problem. Anything less than a total score of 36 might signal a concern, and therefore it is prudent to invite students, parents, and teachers to

comment. Keep in mind that children and adolescents show more vari-
ability of scores than adults, and it is likely that when there is a problem
with the alliance, the score will drop dramatically. Children and adolescents are far less likely to be reluctant to let practitioners know that
something is amiss.

Sometimes clients say that not enough time has passed for them to
know or that the score is the best they can give, and offer no explanation. All answers are okay, and the practitioner needs only to extend the
open invitation to the client to continue the feedback process. Thanking
the client for this feedback and soliciting continued honesty keeps the
avenues of communication open. The practitioner's appreciation of any
negative feedback is a powerful alliance builder. In fact, alliances that
start off negatively but result in practitioner flexibility to client input
tend to be very predictive of a positive outcome. In general:

- A score that is poor and remains poor predicts a negative
  outcome.
- A score that is good and remains good predicts a positive
  outcome.
- A score that is poor or fair and increases predicts a positive
  outcome even more.
- A score that is good and decreases predicts a negative outcome.

The SRS allows the opportunity to fix any alliance problems that are
developing and shows clients that the practitioner does more than give
lip service to honoring the client's perspectives.

> "Let me just take a second here to look at this SRS; it's kind of
> like a thermometer that takes the temperature of our meeting
> today. Wow, great, it looks good, looks like we are on the same
> page, that we are talking about what you think is important
> and you believe today's meeting was right for you. Please let me
> know if I get off track.

> "Let me quickly look at this other form that lets me know how
> you think we are doing. Okay, seems like I am missing the boat
> here. Thanks very much for your honesty and giving me a chance
> to address what I can do differently. Was there something else I
> should have asked you about or should have done to make this
> meeting work better for you? What was missing here?"

Graceful acceptance of alliance problems and a willingness to be flexible speak volumes to the client and usually turn things around. Punctuating this point is the finding that clients reporting alliance problems that are addressed by the practitioner are seven times more likely to achieve successful outcome. Negative scores on the SRS, therefore, are good news and should be celebrated. Practitioners who elicit negative feedback tend to be those with the best effectiveness rates. The SRS/CSRS provides a way to talk about and address alliance difficulties, thereby keeping clients engaged in the intervention process.

Step 5: Checking for Change in Subsequent Meetings

With the feedback culture set, the business of being outcome informed can begin, with the client's view of progress and fit really influencing what happens. Each subsequent meeting compares the current ORS/CORS with the previous one and looks for any changes. The practitioner discusses whether there is an improvement (a move to the right on any scale or an increase in score), a slide (a move to the left or a decrease in score), or no change at all. The scores are used to engage the client in a discussion about progress and, more importantly, what should be done differently if there isn't any progress.

> "[to a student] Wow, your marks on the personal well-being and overall lines really moved—about 4 centimeters to the right each! Your total increased by 8 points to 29 points. That's quite a jump! What happened? How did you pull that off? Where do you think we should go from here?"

> "[to a teacher] Okay, your rating of Kyle improved to a 24, that's 4 points higher than our last meeting. What have you done differently with Kyle that is resulting in this improvement? Was it one of the specific strategies we discussed that you implemented or was it more about the style in which you approached his disruptive behavior, or was it something else?"

If a change has occurred, the practitioner should implement all the ways to empower progress and encourage students, parents, and teachers to take responsibility for a new chapter in their life. If no change has occurred, the scores also invite a discussion, perhaps an even more important one.

"Okay, so things haven't changed since the last time we talked. How do you make sense of that? Should we be doing something different here, or should we continue on course steady as we go? If we are going to stay on the same track, how long should we go before getting worried? When will we know when to say 'when'?"

Again, the idea is to involve the student, parent, or teacher in the process of monitoring progress and the decision about what to do next. The ORS/CORS feedback process is repeated in all meetings, but later ones gain increasing significance and warrant additional action. The precise number of encounters that trigger extra attention or increased discussion is totally dependent on the specific setting in which the service is conducted.

We call these later interactions either *checkpoint conversations* or *last-chance discussions*. Checkpoint conversations are usually conducted at the second meeting and last-chance discussions are initiated in the third meeting. This is simply saying that by the second encounter, clients who receive benefit from the services of a given setting are showing that benefit on the ORS; if change is not noted by meeting 3, then the client is at a significant risk for a negative outcome, based on the average client in that particular setting. These checkpoint and last-chance meeting suggestions are derived from mental health settings involving work with individuals with mild levels of distress. They may or may not fit your school setting. Different settings, (e.g., elementary vs. high school) will have different checkpoints and last-chance numbers. Each setting needs to determine two points during the course of intervention to evaluate whether a client needs a referral or some other change based on a typical successful client in the setting. In Appendix C, a simple method of determining the checkpoint and last-chance meetings for your school setting is discussed.

Here are simple rules for checkpoint conversations and last-chance discussions. Remember that the main idea is to invite students, parents, and teachers into a meaningful exchange of the options that exist to help them meet their goals. If change has not occurred by the checkpoint conversation, the practitioner responds by going through the SRS/CSRS item by item. Alliance problems are a significant contributor to a lack of progress. Sometimes it is useful to say something such as "It doesn't seem like we are getting anywhere. Let me go over the items on this SRS to make sure you are getting exactly what you are looking for from me and our time together." Going through the SRS and eliciting client responses in detail can help the practitioner and client get a better sense of what may or may not be working.

Next, a lack of progress at this stage may indicate that the practitioner needs to try something different, because the client has not reported change in a fashion that is usual for the practitioner or the setting. This can take as many forms as there are clients. The practitioner involves the client in brainstorming options: bringing in different people, a team, another school professional, a different approach; referring to another practitioner, religious advisor, or self-help group—whatever seems to be of value to the client. Any ideas that surface are then implemented, and progress is continually monitored via the ORS.

For example, recall Sean and his teacher's concerns about his classroom behavior. The practitioner and Ms. White discussed Sean's difficulties on two occasions and implemented a behavioral contingency plan, but with no results. The checkpoint conversation revealed Ms. White's belief that there was more going on and that it might be helpful if Sean's mom could be involved. The practitioner called for a meeting, and everyone's ratings of Sean improved markedly by the fourth meeting.

If the practitioner and client have brainstormed and implemented different possibilities and the client has still experienced no change, it is time for the last-chance discussion. As the name implies, there is some urgency for something different because the average successful client at a given setting has already achieved change by this point, and the current client is at significant risk for a negative conclusion. Remember that the purpose of the comparison between this client and the average client attaining a successful outcome is to encourage an open exchange and enable new options for addressing the client's goals. A metaphor we like is that of the practitioner and client driving into a vast desert and running on empty, when a sign appears on the road that says "last chance for gas." The metaphor depicts the necessity of stopping and discussing the implications of continuing without the student, parent, or teacher reaching a desired change.

This is the time when a referral and other available resources should be considered and frankly discussed. If the practitioner has created a feedback culture from the beginning, then this conversation will not be a surprise to the client. Rarely is there justification for continuing to work with clients who have not achieved change in a period typical for the majority of clients seen by a particular practitioner or setting.

It is particularly important to consider a referral because by keeping clients in an ineffective intervention process, practitioners may actually become obstacles to clients making the changes they desire. Research shows that there is no correlation between an intervention with a poor outcome and the likelihood of success in the next intervention encounter. Becoming outcome informed helps practitioners get out of the way and not be impediments to the client's efforts to change.

For example, recall Matt, who was quite distressed about his embarrassing difficulty with urinating in the public restroom. His first practitioner suggested a variety of relaxation and self-talk strategies. The SRS indicated that Matt and the practitioner seemed to click regarding the relationship, but the ORS and Matt's report indicated that no change happened in the problem. The practitioner and Matt brainstormed options in the checkpoint meeting, and fine-tuned Matt's strategies, but by the fourth meeting change still had not occurred. The practitioner openly discussed the lack of change, and Matt and the practitioner concluded that he should talk to someone else. He did, and Matt conquered his problem.

School practitioners, no matter how competent or experienced, cannot be effective with everyone, and other relational fits may work out better for the client. Although some students, parents, and teachers may want to continue in the absence of change, far more do not want to continue when given a graceful way to exit. The ORS/CORS allows practitioners to ask themselves the hard questions and bring clients into the loop about decisions when clients are not, by their own ratings, seeing benefit from services. Outcome management does not help practitioners with the clients they are already effective with; rather, it helps with those who are not benefiting by enabling an open discussion of other options and, in the absence of change, the ability to end honorably and move the client on to a more productive relationship.

OUTCOME-INFORMED INTERVENTION: DOING WHAT WORKS, CHANGING WHAT DOESN'T

Outcome feedback also informs decisions regarding intervention intensity (e.g., intervention or education or outside referral). For example,

Brown et al. (1999) and Miller et al. (2006) found that as many as one third of clients enter with a score that exceeded the clinical cutoff. Encouraging practitioners to adopt a strengths-based or problem-solving approach in lieu of other more intensive strategies or outside referral can serve to maximize engagement while minimizing the risk of client deterioration or intervention overkill. When students are referred for service, or are essentially involuntary clients, and score above the clinical cutoff, the referral source's (teacher or parent) rating can be added to the mix to guide decisions regarding scheduling and intensity. In such cases, the student and practitioner work together to resolve the problem that the referral source has with the client, so that the student can reach the often-stated goal of ending contact with the practitioner.

Consider the issue of intensity of intervention and differences in perspectives with 13-year-old Hannah, who was hastily referred to the school practitioner when her mother, Dorothy, discovered cuts on Hannah's arms and disturbing writings in her school journal. The practitioner began the discussion with Hannah at Dorothy's request.

SCHOOL PRACTITIONER (SP): I have one brief form I want to ask you to do. It's kind of like an anchor point that tells us both where you see yourself right now, and it is a way we can look back and see if we are getting anywhere, if we are on the right track. Just put your name and age and meeting 1—we don't need any of the rest of that junk. Then on these lines, just put a mark where you see yourself on each of those things, how you are doing personally, et cetera, where marks to this end mean you are not doing too well and to this end mean things are going real well. (*Hannah fills out the ORS and the practitioner measures the marks with a centimeter ruler.*) Okay. Great. Things look like they are going pretty well. There are 40 points total and you scored 35.2 out of 40. People usually think their lives are going pretty well when they score that high. Is that true for you?

(*The practitioner administers the ORS and Hannah reports on the ORS that she is doing well. The practitioner already knew, from her record and a brief conversation with teachers, that Hannah was a good student and was infrequently disciplined for talking in class. While the practitioner took the cutting episode very seriously, he also integrated the information from the teachers and Hannah's ORS.*)

HANNAH: Well, yes, but I did cut my arm because of this one boy.

SP: Okay, and you were in a relationship and it didn't go so well?

HANNAH: I like this boy named Jake and I can tell him anything. I can tell him more than my friends who are girls. And he understands it. But I found out he liked me and when I was falling for him I didn't really show it, but now that I am falling for him, he doesn't like me that much so that's why I cut my arm.

SP: You were feeling bad about Jake not falling for you like you fell for him.

HANNAH: Yeah, but then I wrote all my emotions in my school journal and then my mom read it and I got totally mad about it.

SP: No wonder, she's not supposed to be in there fooling around. When did this happen?

HANNAH: Around 3 or 4 days ago. I told her I stopped and I really have stopped and she said it is a progressive addictive disease and you're gonna keep doing it!

SP: That's heavy, isn't it? Wow, she is really freaked out big time. So is part of the job here to figure out a way to convince her you are okay?

HANNAH: (*Nods head "yes."*) Because really I haven't cut myself before or since and the wounds are already about healed. I realized that I cut myself and it really did hurt. Usually, if you are really hurt and you cut yourself it relieves the pain, but it just made my pain worse.

SP: I gotcha. So you heard that sometimes cutting relieves emotional pain but it didn't do that for you.

HANNAH: I read in *Teen People* magazine that girls cut themselves to relieve pain and stress in their lives with razor blades. I couldn't find razor blades so I used a knife. God, that hurt!

SP: I bet, and you found that it didn't relieve the situation at all?

HANNAH: I wanted to try that to see if it would work but it only made it worse. And I tried to explain it to her but she won't listen. No offense, but I don't even need to be here.

SP: What does she tell you when you try to explain that to her?

HANNAH: That it's a sick disease—you are not okay! I say, "Mom, I'm fine," but she won't leave me alone! I don't need a straitjacket.

SP: Let me see (*opening a drawer*), I don't have one anyway. (*Both laugh.*) Your mom is the one we have to convince.

HANNAH: She's like if the counselor tells you not to hang with Jake or Brian, then don't. Until we get everything figured out you are not hanging with any boys. I don't care what she says. These are my friends. She's denying me my friends.

SP: That's probably not going to work anyway because you are going to see your friends at school. But parents get way freaked out about stuff like cutting.

HANNAH: Yeah, but the big problem is that my mom isn't letting me hang out with boys, but that's impossible.

SP: Doesn't she have to get used to that? . . . Unless you join a convent or something.

HANNAH: I will be laughing if you say that!

SP: So you got any ideas about how you can get your mom to not be freaked out?

HANNAH: I tried to convince her and it always comes out as yelling and screaming at each other—she doesn't listen—she says, "You're not going to hang out with those boys!" (*in a sarcastic tone*) Shut up!

SP: And your mom wants you to stop seeing these boys all together?

HANNAH: And I don't want to—that's impossible. She just won't understand and she won't take "no" for an answer. I need someone to make her understand.

SP: So that's what you want me to do? (*Hannah nods.*) . . . Now that you have some distance from this cutting thing, what do you think?

HANNAH: It hurt and I didn't like it, like it didn't work, and when I read over my school journal, I was like, "What was I thinking?" I liked him but I don't like him that much anymore.

SP: Would anybody be worth doing that over?

HANNAH: No!

The school practitioner pursued the cutting episode and Hannah's thoughts about it. Hannah didn't see a problem with the cutting, but her mother obviously had a different perspective. The only thing that Hannah was interested in was convincing her mom that she should be able to see her friends who are boys. Although more dramatic, Hannah's predicament fits the common scenario of differing goals between students and adults. As discussed in Chapter 2, the school practitioner takes what Hannah wants at face value knowing that working on client goals is a critical element of the alliance.

Obviously, Dorothy's perspective is paramount. If Dorothy painted a different picture of the cutting, for example, if the cutting was not an isolated incident, then different action would likely be warranted. Talking to Dorothy alone, the practitioner administers and totals Dorothy's rating of Hannah on the ORS and the conversation begins.

SP: Each of these lines is 10 centimeters long, for a total of 40, and you scored Hannah a 32.4. The cutoff score for adolescents is 28, which just means that people who rate themselves or others under that are in enough distress to talk to someone like me, versus people who are not. So your score says that you think Hannah is doing pretty well.

DOROTHY: She's not doing that bad. It's just what she did.

SP: So it is this particular event that has frightened you enough to call me, and that makes total sense to me. As a parent I know I would be very frightened by this as well. And your concern about this cutting accounts for your mark on the Individually line, that mark of 6.8?

DOROTHY: Yes, exactly. I am a mess over that. When I read her school journal, I couldn't believe what I read. And all over this boy! I went totally ballistic! I can't tell you how much trouble I got in with boys when I was about her age. I don't want her to wind up the same way. . . . So I grounded her from talking to boys on the phone and seeing them after school to skateboard until I figure out what's going on and hear what you think about it. She has friends, but I'd rather they be more girls. She does have girlfriends though.

SP: No wonder you are a mess! I think any parent in their right mind would be. This was an extreme reaction to a relationship not working out, and the cutting itself—just about a parent's worse nightmare.

DOROTHY: That's for sure.

SP: So what you are looking for from me is an opinion about this cutting episode, and, let me know if I am not getting this, some assurance that Hannah is okay.

DOROTHY: Exactly. So what do you think?

SP: Well, Hannah is a great kid. She is fiercely independent, in a good way, and her teachers tell me she really is not a follower but a kid who likes to make up her own mind. I was impressed with her for a lot of reasons, but in particular about her ability to articulate herself and her ability to stand up for what she believes.

DOROTHY: Like you say, she says what she feels and she is very independent.

SP: You have done a lot right with her.

DOROTHY: Thank you. That's my problem—I don't give myself much credit . . . I have more problems than she does, but that's okay, I can handle that.

SP: When you look at her you ought to give yourself credit—you've done great things with her and you have a great relationship. And yes, I think she is okay—there are many sides of this cutting episode but it does appear to be an isolated incident that Hannah and you can reflect about, put in proper perspective, keep an eye on, but move on.

DOROTHY: That's what I thought, but I wasn't sure.

The school practitioner validated Dorothy's concerns and her strengths, and addressed her reason for making the appointment. The ORS provided a snapshot of Dorothy's perspective of Hannah and confirmed that Dorothy thought that Hannah was doing pretty well despite the recent cutting. Had Dorothy reported other concerns and scored Hannah below the cutoff (e.g., that Hannah was depressed or was engaged in any dangerous behaviors), then the practitioner would have considered other options including a referral to outside providers. The practitioner ended the meeting by bringing Hannah and Dorothy in together. The practitioner planned to set a follow-up meeting to negotiate Hannah's desire to have her right to see boys reinstated, as well as highlight how both had worked through the cutting episode.

SP: I am impressed with both of you. You two are a great combination. Your mom has done a lot right with you. You are independent and strong-willed. And I was telling your mom that can be a great pain in the neck to a parent!

HANNAH: I like him!

DOROTHY: Me too.

SP: But that also can be a great thing. You are your own thinker. But you had this thing happen which is going to freak out any parent and should, and you need to work it through and see what it is about and make sense of it, so you both can go on with things. And that's what I had in mind—if that seems like a reasonable thing for both of you?

DOROTHY: Yes it does. (*Hannah nods.*)

HANNAH: Did you make a decision about the boys and stuff?

SP: I was planning on talking about that in the next meeting. I know you two have differences of opinion about that and obviously are on real different sides to that issue.

DOROTHY: Not real different sides.

HANNAH: Yes we are!

DOROTHY: No (*talking to Hannah*). Because we are not. Well I let her— she's been hanging with the boys. She also has girlfriends, but I just don't like what I read and what you were dealing with!

HANNAH: That's how I WAS!

DOROTHY: That day?

HANNAH: That day—thank you!

DOROTHY: That's what I needed to know.

HANNAH: Well, it's hard to talk to you when you are so freaked out.

DOROTHY: But you don't talk to me when it comes to boys, you don't tell me what is deep down. I've always told you that you could come to me and talk to me.

HANNAH: My feelings deep down: I still sort of like Jake, but I realize when I cut myself it was only making the pain worse.

DOROTHY: You do understand that what you did was wrong?

HANNAH: Yeah, but it doesn't mean you can keep me from my friends.

DOROTHY: No, okay.

HANNAH: Thank you!

SP: This is great! You are working at understanding each other and it goes both ways.

DOROTHY: You know I love you.

HANNAH: Duh, you don't love me and never cared about me! (*All laugh.*)

SP: Great. Sounds like you have come to an agreement about the boy issue. . . . Would you both fill out one more form for me? This gets at how the meeting went today. It's just a way for me to get feedback so I can do something different if I need to. (*Administers the SRS.*)

HANNAH: All 10's. . . . You're cool!

DOROTHY: Me too.

SP: Great. Thanks, I appreciate it. If anything comes up please let me know so I am in line with what you think should be happening.

It is just these unexpected events that make this work fun. Although the practitioner was planning on negotiating Hannah's goals in the next meeting, Hannah and Dorothy spontaneously resolved the issue. Dorothy heard what she needed to hear to have her fears assuaged, and reinstituted Hannah's boy privileges. The ORS provided guidance about the intensity of intervention as well as a road map to the differing perspectives of Dorothy and Hannah. Dorothy followed up by telephone, reporting that things were going well and that she didn't think another appointment was necessary. The practitioner touched base with Dorothy and Hannah one additional time, as well as with Hannah's teachers.

Failing Successfully: An Honorable Conclusion

Carrie had everything going for her in her senior year. She was captain of the volleyball team and valedictorian of her class and already was accepted to a prestigious university. But then the bottom fell out; she started experiencing inexplicable and very frightening anxiety attacks. Her family doctor, believing that Carrie was depressed, prescribed an antidepressant, but Carrie thought the drug made her feel jumpy and stopped taking it. Over her high school years, Carrie had periodically talked to her school practitioner about a variety of issues. Given the foundation of their relationship, Carrie asked him if they could meet regularly to resolve the panic attack problem. In the meantime, Carrie became quite distraught. Her schoolwork suffered and she feared for her ability to go away to college. Carrie scored a 12 on the ORS, indicating a high level of distress.

Carrie and the practitioner discussed how the panic episodes threatened everything she had always dreamed of and worked so hard to prepare for. They also discussed self-esteem issues and a variety of reasons that could account for the panic. But nothing happened—no change was reflected on the ORS. In meeting 2, the practitioner conducted the checkpoint conversation and went over the SRS. Confirming that the relationship itself could not be any better, Carrie also mentioned that she wanted some specific things to do when faced with an impending attack. The practitioner responded to the feedback and outlined a plan for Carrie to monitor her anxiety levels, and then use imagery and relaxation when she noted high levels. But after a few weeks of implementation and fine-tuning, as well as involving Carrie's dad, no change ensued. Now at meeting 4, Carrie was at high risk for a negative outcome: Despite the good relationship, her ORS score remained a paltry 12.

It was time for the last-chance discussion. The practitioner explained that the lack of change had nothing to do with either of them, that they had both tried their best, and that for whatever reason, it just wasn't the right mix for change. They discussed the possibility of Carrie seeing someone else, and a referral was made to a community practitioner who was willing to continue monitoring outcome in the way that Carrie had become accustomed, and who would honor Carrie's wishes regarding no medication.

By session 4 with the community therapist, Carrie had an ORS score of 19 and had enrolled in a class at a local university to make up for her lost time at school. Moreover, she continued those changes and was able to attend college when fall classes began. By getting out of Carrie's way and allowing himself to "fail successfully," the school practitioner set the stage for Carrie to move on with her life.

We cannot be effective with everyone. Other relational fits may work out better for the client. Becoming outcome-informed allows us to ask the hard questions when clients are not, by their own ratings, seeing benefit from our services, and provides a way to bring clients into the loop of the decision-making process.

OUTCOME AND THE FUTURE: IMAGINE . . .

For most of the history of the field, practitioners have been trained to attribute a lack of progress either to the client (mainly), to themselves, or to the intervention offered. Common sense suggests that it is simply not possible for practitioners to form successful working relationships with every person they encounter. However, intervention can be considered successful both when clients achieve change and when, in the absence of change, the practitioner works with the client to get out of the way.

Becoming outcome informed is simple and straightforward, and could potentially unify the field around the common goal of change. Unlike the product-oriented efforts the field has employed thus far, outcome management results in significant improvements in effectiveness. Liberated from the traditional focus on product or technique, practitioners would be better able to achieve what they always claimed to have been in the business of doing—assisting change.

Imagine clients involved in every aspect of intervention and receiving services based on their views of change, and using their feedback to guide all decisions. Imagine less emphasis on diagnostic workups or other assessments that have little relevance to outcome. Imagine for the first time school professionals having proof of the effectiveness and value of their day-to-day work. Imagine no longer gaining acceptance by adopting the questionable language and practices of the medical profession (e.g., the DSM, prescriptive interventions). It's easy if you try.

CHAPTER 5

♦ ♦ ♦

Brief Intervention
Solution Building

♦

This is the first of two chapters illustrating brief intervention with full-length client examples. Chapter 5 highlights the solution-building style of interviewing, showing how practitioners can flexibly apply the three-E method of utilizing exceptions. This chapter also demonstrates how students, teachers, and parents can be enlisted in a simple process of monitoring the outcome and fit of services. The intervention process is presented in the following sections: (1) referral and background information, (2) establishing client-directed partnerships, (3) the three-step method of solution building, and (4) monitoring and empowering intervention outcomes.

REFERRAL AND BACKGROUND INFORMATION

Derek, a 10th-grade student, was referred for services by his teachers and the school principal due to major concerns about disruptive classroom behavior and minimal assignment completion. He was in a special education program for students with learning disabilities. The referral was made in mid-October, following the first quarter grading period. Derek was described as resistant, defiant, oppositional, and apathetic. The referral form portrayed a dismal picture of Derek and his prospects for change, along with the teachers' sense of frustration.

Records revealed a history of family and school problems. Derek had been in several foster homes and two residential facilities for children with behavior problems. Prior to enrolling in the learning disabilities program, he participated in programs for students with emotional–behavioral disabilities. Community social services was monitoring Derek's progress, and he and his father were on a waiting list for family counseling. Because of increased behavior problems at school, a foster home or residential placement was under consideration.

ESTABLISHING CLIENT-DIRECTED PARTNERSHIPS

Assessment is traditionally viewed as a separate and distinct process from intervention: First you assess and diagnose, and then you intervene. Not so here, where assessment is part and parcel of client-directed partnerships and intervention itself. Assessment no longer precedes and dictates intervention; Rather, it weaves in and out of the helping process. As you read through this chapter, notice how client-directed partnerships are established with all the major people involved in the problem.

First Interview with Teachers

Derek's teachers were interviewed first because they initiated the request for intervention assistance. Each teacher completed a short referral form about a week before the first interview. The following dialogue is taken from the first interview with the two teachers expressing the most concerns: Mr. Roth (math) and Ms. Calhoun (English). The practitioner (1) explains his desire to be useful and highlights the importance of their feedback, (2) discusses the ORS and SRS, (3) validates their frustrations and perceptions, and (4) listens for heroic stories.

SCHOOL PRACTITIONER (SP): I appreciate both of you taking the time to be here. I know it's really hard to break away during the school day to meet like this. In the e-mail that I sent you last week to schedule this meeting, I mentioned that I want be as helpful as possible in helping to turn things around with this situation. In order to do that, I'll occasionally ask you how things are going with Derek, how our meetings are working for you, and what I can do to make myself and our meetings as useful as possible. Does that sound okay?

MR. ROTH: That's fine.

MS. CALHOUN: Yes.

SP: Thanks. I appreciate that. You're the ones who are working with Derek every day and your feedback is very important to me. I like to use a couple of short forms to get your impressions about how Derek is doing and how useful our meetings are for you. This first form is called the Outcome Rating Scale, or ORS, and it gives a quick sense of how Derek is doing in your opinion as well as an anchor point to compare our progress to. (*Administers and scores the ORS.*) Let's start with you, Ms. Calhoun.

Ms. Calhoun's total score for Derek on the ORS was 15.5; her lower ratings respectively were 5.3 (Individually) and 2.7 (Socially—the school scale). Similarly, Mr. Roth's ratings put Derek at a total score of 14.8 with the same two scales representing the lower ratings (Individually, 4.2; Socially, 3.3).

SP: (*looking over the ORS forms*) I can see that both of you have some serious concerns about how things are going for Derek right now, especially at school. The way this measure works is that there are four 10-centimeter lines that add to a total score of 40. The cutoff score for adolescents, or the number that separates those who are struggling enough to be involved in some kind of intervention from those who are not, is 28. You both scored Derek well below that number, and that simply says that we are all in the right place right now, trying to figure what we can do to help him get on track. Does that make sense?

MS. CALHOUN AND MR. ROTH: Yes.

SP: It would help me to catch up on things to hear from both of you about what Derek is doing or not doing in your class that concerns you the most. Who's first?

MR. ROTH: Where do I start? (*some laughter*) Seriously, there are so many problems. He's late to class about three times a week. When he gets there, I have to tell him at least once to get his book out. Never has homework. His behavior is the pits. He talks out whenever he feels like it, calls across the room to other students, threatens other kids. I've sent him out for cussing. And these aren't words under his breath. Everybody can hear them, including people in the hallway. Those are the biggest problems in my class.

SP: What other things is he doing, or not doing, that's causing problems in your class? [Seeks a clear description of the problem from Mr. Roth's perspective.]

MR. ROTH: Well, as far as "not doing," I haven't seen him work on anything in class more than a minute or so.

SP: What kinds of things?

MR. ROTH: Mostly it's problem sheets.

SP: What are problem sheets?

MR. ROTH: I call them problem sheets and they do them three or four times a week. A lot of times, he doesn't even attempt to do it.

SP: Do you think he has the math skills to do the sheets?

MR. ROTH: I think he can do it. To be honest, he's done so little it's hard to say.

SP: Well, I can see why you're frustrated. There's a bunch of stuff going on here. Like you said earlier, where do you start? Now let me make sure I'm getting this right (*picking up Mr. Roth's ORS*), the problems you talked about, the lateness, the talking out, the not doing work . . . do those problems account for your mark on this [Socially] line?

MR. ROTH: Yes, and also partly on the first line [Individually] because I see the behavior problems as more about him personally.

SP: Okay, makes sense. What do you think you would notice first if your mark on either the Individually line or the Socially line moved just 1 centimeter to the right? [The practitioner (1) validates Mr. Roth's frustration and perception of multiple problems by mirroring his earlier words ("Where do I start?") and (2) connects the marks on the ORS to his experience of Derek in the classroom and what change might look like.]

MR. ROTH: Definitely the behavior would change. I would notice that in a heartbeat. He would just stop being so surly and angry about everything . . . something needs to happen. I don't see how he can stay in my class, or this program, unless he gets his act together fast.

MS. CALHOUN: I agree. His behavior is my biggest concern, although it's real disruptive to the class when he comes in late because he usually talks to someone in the hall real loud, then comes in and plops in his seat, taps on his desk, says something rude to a student. Stuff like that really disrupts things when you're just starting a lesson or explaining an assignment. Then he mutters stuff like "This sucks" or "This is stupid" under his breath when I give them an assignment.

SP: When he comes in late, what happens?

MS. CALHOUN: You mean what does he do next?

SP: Him, you, other students. Yeah. I'm just trying to get a picture of what it looks like when this happens. Like if I were a fly on the wall, what would I see first, then next, and so on, after he comes in the room late? [In addition to obtaining a concrete description, clarifying previous solution attempts can be helpful if exceptions do not emerge.]

MS. CALHOUN: Well, usually I tell him he'll need an admit slip from the Discipline Office by the end of the day for being late. He just sighs or shrugs his shoulders. He's walked out a couple times, usually muttering something under his breath about the school or me. I try to ignore some of it, but it's so loud sometimes that I can't. I also don't want all the other students thinking they can get away with the same kind of stuff. He flies off the handle so easy.

SP: I see what you mean. It's like a Catch-22. You're darned if you do and darned if you don't. [These comments enhance the alliance by validating Ms. Calhoun's perceptions and predicament.]

MS. CALHOUN: Exactly. I don't know what to do. And I can't teach 18 other students with all this going on.

SP: What else have you tried?

MS. CALHOUN: I've talked with him a couple times to try and figure out why he's so angry.

SP: How did that work?

MS. CALHOUN: Well, he's better one to one, but he just kind of shrugged and said he didn't know why he did this stuff. I told him he was heading for more problems unless something changed.

SP: Did his behavior change at all after you talked to him?

MS. CALHOUN: Not really. Maybe a little, but it didn't last.

SP: You mentioned anger before. Could you tell me what you mean? [This question explores Ms. Calhoun's theory of the problem.]

MS. CALHOUN: I don't know what else it could be. He just seems so angry. I just figured, maybe if he talked about it, you know, got it out, maybe he'd be better. He wouldn't think we were so against him.

SP: I see what you mean. I can check that out when I meet with him. Now let me see if I am getting this. Your marks on the ORS here (*picking up the form*), on the Individually line, is that this anger, disruption, and stuff you are talking about?

MS. CALHOUN: Yes.

SP: Okay, and the work itself. How much work does he do in English class?

MS. CALHOUN: Not much. Sometimes he'll come in and get his paper out and start working. Most of the time he comes in and sits there, says something rude to another student, or lays his head on the desk. [The practitioner connects Ms. Calhoun's description of Derek's anger to her mark on the Individually line so that any movement of that mark will signify changes. The comment that Derek "sometimes" does work is a small but potentially important exception. Listening for exceptions paves the way for a competing and more hopeful story that stands in contrast to the prevailing description of Derek. Next, the practitioner explores the conditions surrounding this exception.]

SP: What's different about those times when he gets his paper out and does more work?

MS. CALHOUN: I wish I knew (*laughs*).

SP: Yeah. If you knew, you'd be on *Oprah*, right?

MS. CALHOUN: Right.

SP: I mean, I wonder whether it makes a difference whether it's a certain type of assignment, or maybe he's sitting in a different spot, something like that. I don't know. Can you think of anything like that that might give us a clue about what's going on when he gets his paper out?

MS. CALHOUN: No. Not really. Not offhand.

SP: What would you think of observing things during the times when he does a little better in classroom behavior or assignments? Things like what type of assignment it is, who he's sitting next to, and anything else you think might be important. [This task is useful in two respects. First, it does not require much time or change in classroom routine. Second, it encourages the discovery of exceptions and more positive stories about Derek in the eyes of his teachers.]

MS. CALHOUN: I'll try anything that will help.

SP: Mr. Roth, would it be possible to make these kind of observations in your class?

MR. ROTH: I guess so. I can try, but I don't want to see this thing carried out for months, and us be sitting here again scratching our heads wondering what to do, you know?

SP: Yeah. I think things have reached a point where everybody's kind of at wits' end, including Mr. Becker [the school principal]. I'm going to call Derek's father and tell him about our meeting, ask for any input and suggestions he might have. I'll also meet with Derek. I have to say, as frustrated as you all are, dealing with this day in and day out, it's impressive to me that you're still willing to meet to even discuss it, much less to consider ways to change it. Some people would have given up long ago. He is lucky to have you in his corner trying to improve things and help make things better for him at school. [The practitioner validates the teachers' perseverance and commitment to Derek.] Before you go, I'd appreciate you taking just a minute to complete another short survey about our meeting today. This form (*handing them the SRS*) is called the Session Rating Scale, or SRS. It's set up just like the other form with four questions and a line for you to answer each question. As I said when we started, I want to make sure that I'm being useful to you and that these meetings are working the way you want them to. Your feedback on this form will tell me how the meeting worked for you and what I can do to be as helpful as possible.

The practitioner quickly scored the SRS forms, noting any domain that fell more than 1 centimeter to the left of a perfect 10. Ms. Calhoun scored a total 38.2, with all scores above 9, while Mr. Roth scored a total 36, but only an 8.2 on Goals and Topics. Recall from Chapter 4 that a total score of 36 or below should be discussed, whereas a score of 37 or above suggests, but does not guarantee, an effective fit between the practitioner's approach and the client. Recall also that a negative SRS score provides far more helpful information than a positive score because it allows the practitioner to address emerging alliance problems.

SP: *(looking at the ratings)* Great. It looks like we're pretty much on the same page and that the meeting was useful to both you. Mr. Roth, you marked the Goals and Topics item a little lower than the others. Is there something that you wanted to address in more detail or that we skipped over too lightly in this meeting?

MR. ROTH: Well, I know we can't cover everything in 30 minutes, but I'd like to see if some testing could be done to see if he has the ability to do what we're asking him to do?

SP: What type of testing are you thinking of?

MR. ROTH: Well, I'm not sure. I guess IQ testing. What do you think?

SP: I'll check into this. I'd like to see what's already been done in the testing area, when it's been done, look at the results, and so forth. I could get back to you with this information and we could discuss it further in a few days. How is that for you?

MR. ROTH: That's fine.

SP: Okay. Thanks for the feedback and for taking the time to catch me up on things today.

Derek's other teachers reported similar perceptions and concerns except for Ms. Smith, who told a different story. She reported that he was rarely rude in her social studies class. When asked about why his behavior was more acceptable in her class, Ms. Smith said that she occasionally joked with Derek and he liked it. This competing story offered a useful exception.

First Interview with Mr. Brown (Derek's Father)

When Derek's father was called, he said that he was working double shifts and could not talk for long. When the practitioner offered to call at a different time, Mr. Brown said that now was as good as any. To respect the time constraints, the practitioner did not administer the ORS, but asked Mr. Brown to rate how well school was going for Derek on a scale of 1 to 10. He replied, "between 2 and 3."

When asked for his advice on how to help Derek, Mr. Brown stated that he had tried talking to Derek and withholding privileges. Withholding privileges made things worse. The talks helped the two of them get along for a few days but did not change things at school. Mr. Brown said it was difficult for him to help Derek on school matters because he worked the second shift and was not available for Derek as often as he would like. He shared his frustration and added that he was open to anything the practitioner might suggest. Acknowledging that Mr. Brown ultimately knows best, the practitioner encouraged him to try something different.

Before hanging up, the practitioner asked if there was anything else he could do. Mr. Brown requested that the practitioner meet with Derek and try to help him in school. He also wanted Derek to continue living with him instead of being placed outside the home. The practitioner validated Mr. Brown for trying different ways to help Derek and for hanging in there.

First Interview with Derek

Derek hunkered down in the chair, pulled his hat over his forehead, and said, "This school sucks."

DEREK: You can't make me talk about anything if I don't want to. They can't either.

SP: You are right about that! When you say they, who do you mean?

DEREK: (*Shrugs shoulders.*)

SP: Your teachers?

DEREK: (*Nods head "yes."*)

SP: Do you have an idea why they asked me to talk with you?

DEREK: (*Shrugs shoulders and shakes head, indicating "no."*)

SP: Well, some of your teachers want to see changes in things like getting to class on time and doing some more work in class. Does that surprise you any?

DEREK: (*Shakes head, indicating "no."*)

SP: Would you prefer me to ask "yes-or-no" type questions so that you can just nod your head to answer if you don't feel like talking? [The practitioner adjusts to the client instead of expecting the client to adjust to him.]

DEREK: I can talk.

SP: Okay. Can you help me out with this form? Your teachers filled one out about you and I'd like to get your take on how things are going for you. This is one way I can make sure that you have a say in things along with your teachers. And your answers will also help us see if we're on the right track here, to see how things are going for you during our work together, and to let us know if we need to change anything to make it better. (*Hands Derek the ORS and explains it to him, taking time to make sure Derek understands.*) Make sense?

DEREK: Yes.

SP: Great. Go ahead and mark the lines and ask me questions if you have them as you're going through it. (*Derek rates the ORS: Individually [7.3]; Interpersonally [4.6]; Socially [2.1]; Overall [5]; Total = 19.*) These scores tell me that things are pretty tough for you right now, especially at school and home. People who score under 28 tend to be saying that life is on rough side right now, and for you school seems particularly bad. I can see why you say that school sucks . . . that's pretty much what your score says too.

DEREK: Yeah.

SP: Okay. So what do you think needs to happen to make your mark on that school line move to the right a bit?

DEREK: I want to get out of this stupid school.

SP: Have you figured out a way to do that?

DEREK: (*Looks at the practitioner for the first time and appears sur-*

prised by the question.) No. Well, they suspend me sometimes, but it just lasts for a few days, like 2 days or something.

SP: Would you like it to last longer? [The practitioner neither argues with Derek nor makes any assumptions about his goals or perceptions. This stands in stark contrast to the usual lectures and previous interactions with adults, thereby engaging Derek and building the alliance.]

DEREK: Well, kind of, but not really because if I get kicked out, I could get in a lot of trouble.

(*Derek becomes more talkative as the conversation unfolds. He describes previous foster homes and treatment facilities, and emphatically states that he wants to stay with his father instead of being "sent away again to one of those places."*)

SP: What needs to happen so you won't get sent away?

DEREK: I don't know. I guess if I stop getting in trouble here.

SP: What else would help you stay where you're at?

DEREK: I don't know. They [Social Services caseworkers] tell me I'll get sent away if I keep getting in trouble at school.

SP: So what can you do at school to help you stay where you're at?

DEREK: Well, I guess that stuff they said about being late to class and talking and stuff.

SP: You mean the stuff your teachers said was causing problems?

DEREK: Yeah.

SP: And we would likely see your mark here on the school line move to the right if those things got better?

DEREK: Yeah.

THE THREE-STEP METHOD OF SOLUTION BUILDING

The three E's of solution building were helpful in the work with Derek: (1) *eliciting* exceptions, (2) *elaborating* the details, and (3) *expanding* the exception.

Step 1: Eliciting

It is often necessary to ask questions to elicit exceptions. In this portion of the interview, the practitioner discovers a potentially useful exception by asking Derek about the times when he does not get in trouble.

SP: So, you actually want to stay in school?

DEREK: Yeah. I don't want to get sent away.

SP: That makes sense. Do you want to see if we can come up with things that might help you not get sent away so you can stay with your father and stay in school?

DEREK: Yeah. Like what?

SP: I don't know. Tell me about the times at school when you don't get in trouble as much.

DEREK: I never get in trouble, well (*laughs*), not a lot, in Ms. Smith's class.

SP: Really?

DEREK: Yeah.

SP: What subject do you have Ms. Smith for?

DEREK: Social studies.

SP: Hmm. That's interesting.

Step 2: Elaborating

Next, the details of this exception are explored with Derek. These instances of liberation from the problem, no matter how small or infrequent, add to a more hopeful story about Derek and the prospects of change.

SP: What's so different about Ms. Smith's class than your other classes?

DEREK: I don't know, she's nicer. We get along good.

SP: What exactly does she do that's nicer?

DEREK: I don't know, she's just nice. She says "hi" to me when I come to class. She doesn't hassle me like the other teachers. We got some real jerk teachers in this school.

SP: That's impressive that you would notice her saying "hi" when some students don't notice things like that. It's great that you're able to pick up on things like that. Some students wouldn't even notice that. What else does she do that's nice? [The practitioner follows Derek's lead by commenting on his response to Ms. Smith's friendly greeting. This validates his perceptive and sensitive side, adding yet another positive layer to the emerging story of Derek.]

DEREK: She checks up on me to see how I'm doing on stuff. Like, she'll walk by my desk and ask if I need help on anything.

SP: What else?

DEREK: I guess that's it.

SP: How about her class, or the stuff you study in social studies. Do you like social studies?

DEREK: Not really. It's pretty boring.

SP: What else is different about Ms. Smith, or her class, or the kind of work you do in her class?

DEREK: The work is easier in her class, plus she helps you with it. She doesn't give you as much stuff to do. It's, like, one sheet.

Teacher interviews indicated that Derek had not completed an assignment for the past month in any class except Ms. Smith's. The details of this exception are that (1) Ms. Smith greeted him when he entered the class; (2) she gave him "easier work"; and (3) she checked in with him and helped him as needed.

Several competing stories of Derek emerged within 30 minutes of conversation: (1) the story of family loyalty and a strong father–son bond, (2) the story of a perceptive and responsive person, and (3) the story of a student capable of behaving effectively. Elaborating exceptions also invites clients to acknowledge their role in the changes.

SP: So how are you different in Ms. Smith's class? How is it that you manage to pretty much stay out of trouble in that class?

DEREK: I just do my work. I like the class, so I do my work.

SP: More than you do in other classes?

DEREK: A lot more.

SP: Do you get to class on time more in Ms. Smith's than in your other classes?

DEREK: Yeah. She's real nice. She stands by the door and says "hi" to everybody that comes in. See, that's what I mean, she's nicer.

SP: Okay. She's nicer, but you also do things different in her class, right? You're different. I mean you act different, in her class, right?

DEREK: Right.

SP: How are you different there?

DEREK: I don't know, I guess I just get there on time.

SP: What do you mean?

DEREK: You know, I get there before the late bell rings. So I don't get sent out for being late.

SP: Wow. That must be hard for you to do, because you've been late for classes a lot this year. [This conversation reinforces the story of Derek as a conscientious student who cares about being on time for class.]

DEREK: Yeah.

SP: I've met some students who "say" they want to be on time, but when it comes to actually doing it, they fall short. How do you get yourself there on time when there are so many distractions and reasons to be late?

DEREK: I just go to my locker right from lunch, and go straight to the class.

SP: Do you go straight to the other classes?

DEREK: (*Laughs.*) No. I'll see some people in the hall and talk and stuff.

SP: This is really wild. This is really something. So it's not like it's something you can't do, like you can't get there in time to classes, but it's more like a choice or something you decide on. Is that true?

DEREK: Yeah. If I want to go, I go. I just usually don't feel like going to class.

SP: Well, I imagine it's still hard to do even if you want to, isn't it?

DEREK: A little. I mean, I just don't like the other classes, so I'm late and I screw off more.

SP: Do you think being on time, paying attention better, stuff like that, more like you're doing in social studies, is helping your chances of staying where you're at with your dad and not getting sent to another one of those places?

[The conversation culminates with Derek making the connection between his successful classroom behavior and his desire to stay with his father.]

DEREK: I think if I do more stuff like come to class and be on time it will help.

SP: So it's like whatever you're doing in Ms. Smith's class is helping you not get sent away, helping you stay in school and do decent work so that you won't get sent away. Is that true?

DEREK: Yeah.

Step 3: Expanding

Elaborating exceptions sets the stage for expanding their presence at school.

SP: I wonder how you could do some of that same stuff in your other classes?

DEREK: I guess I could just do it.

SP: It seems to me like it would be really hard to all of a sudden change that quick. What do you think?

DEREK: I don't know. Yeah, maybe.

SP: Would you be willing to try doing "Ms. Smith behavior" in one of your other classes?

DEREK: I get it. I see what you mean. So I could come to English class on time and behave without screwing around and stuff.

SP: Yeah. What do you think about that?

DEREK: I think I can do it. I could do it in my other classes, too.

SP: Well, it's up to you, but that's a big change. You don't want to bite off more than you can chew, you know.

This conversation allows Derek to save face if he is unsuccessful and to decide how quickly and in what classes he wants to change. Derek volunteered to be on time and do more work in English and history class. Further actions included shortening hallway conversations and taking more notes.

The practitioner introduces the SRS during the last 5 minutes of the meeting.

SP: Derek, you really did great in this meeting. You helped me understand things better. I learned a lot about how things are going for you at school. You also taught me what you're doing in Ms. Smith's class that's working for you and making things better in that class. How did this meeting work for you?

DEREK: What do you mean?

SP: I mean, did our talk here help you any?

DEREK: Yeah, it helped.

SP: That's good, because I want to be useful to you. That's my job here. The only way I can tell if I'm helping is to ask you. It doesn't matter what I think is helpful. The only thing that matters is what you think. Does that make sense?

DEREK: Yes.

SP: I know I've worked you pretty hard here, Derek, but I wanted to ask if you would be willing to answer a few more quick questions for me.

DEREK: Sure.

SP: We'll see how it goes this week when you try some of these new things at school. This is the other form (*handing Derek the SRS*) that I'd appreciate you marking to tell me how the meeting went for you. This form tells me what I need to do to be helpful to you and to make our meetings work the way you want them to. It's a lot like the other form. It has four questions and a line for each question. You just read each question and mark the line to show your answer just like you did on the other sheet. Okay? (*Derek rates the SRS and his total score is 34.2.*) Okay. Looks like I listened okay, but you wanted to talk about something else or that something was missing from the meeting. What would have made the meeting better for you?

DEREK: It was good.

[Young people are rarely asked for their opinion and may be reluctant to share feedback about an adult. The practitioner gently coaxes him to clarify his lower SRS ratings on the Goals and Topics and Overall categories.]

SP: I really need your help on this, Derek. You won't hurt my feelings because I want to be useful and the only way I can do that is for you to tell me. I ask people these questions all the time and it always helps me when they tell me how to make the meetings better. So, it seems like maybe something was missing. What else could we have talked about or done in the meeting to make things better for you?

DEREK: It was okay, like I said, it's just that it seems like everybody's always talking to me about school and behavior and stuff like that. I get tired of it, you know?

SP: Yeah. I can see how it would get real old talking about school all the time, people asking you a bunch of questions, stuff like that.

DEREK: I know people care and everything. But like you said, it gets old. It's like, "Leave me alone."

SP: Well, maybe next time we meet we can talk about something besides just school. What other things would you like to talk to me about?

DEREK: Anything, like fishing, dirt bikes, music.

SP: We can talk about one of those things or all of them next time we meet. I mean, I still need to check with you about how school is going because I want to help you stay here instead of being sent to a foster home. But we can also talk about other things, too.

DEREK: Do you know anything about fishing and dirt bikes?

SP: More about music and fishing than dirt bikes. But I've been on some dirt bikes and maybe you could teach me some things about that. We can talk about some of that next time instead of spending the whole time on school, okay?

DEREK: Okay.

SP: I'd like to meet again in about a week to see how things are going. Is that okay with you?

DEREK: Yeah, that's fine.

SP: Great. I'm here on Wednesday afternoon. Will that work?

DEREK: Yes.

SP: It was good talking with you, Derek. I really appreciate you hanging in there with me for the whole meeting.

Expanding Exceptions with Teachers

Building on the meeting with Derek, each teacher was asked to consider the strategies Derek found helpful—greeting him in a friendly way, breaking his work into smaller units, and checking if he needs help. Every teacher agreed to try at least one of the strategies. Ms. Calhoun and Mr. Roth also agreed to rate Derek's progress on the ORS every 2 weeks.

MONITORING AND EMPOWERING
INTERVENTION OUTCOMES

Derek improved his school behavior following the first interview. The practitioner and Derek spoke briefly a couple of times in the hallway, but it was 4 weeks after the initial interview that another meeting took place. Recall that during the discussion of Derek's SRS, he said that he wanted to talk about something else besides school. The practitioner reminded Derek of this discussion and asked what other topic he wanted to discuss. After 10 minutes of spirited exchange about dirt-biking, the conversation shifted to how things were going for Derek at school and elsewhere.

SP: I've got these forms from your teachers that I want to show you in a minute. But first, I need you to complete it (*handing Derek the ORS*). [Derek's ORS totals 32.4.] Wow, look at these ratings! They've really gone up from the first time we met. In fact, you rated every area as being better now than it was the first time we met back in October. Your total score is up over 13 points. Look at this (*showing Derek his ORS from October*). Wow, look at this school line—all the way up to a whopping 8.3. Let's check out what your teachers rated to see how they're seeing things these days. [The practitioner and Derek review his teachers' recent ORS ratings, which are consistently higher than when services were initiated.] These ratings are going way up, too. What's going on here, Derek?

DEREK: Doing my work. I'm trying instead of just sitting there. I'm not messing with other kids as much.

SP: This is pretty different than the way it used to be, isn't it?

DEREK: Yeah, a lot different. You can ask the principal of my school last year how much trouble I've been in there. Man, all the time.

SP: You were in trouble a lot down there?

DEREK: All the time. I'd get suspended for 3 days. Get suspended, come back, get suspended again.

SP: When's the last time you've been suspended up here?

DEREK: Uh, September. Yeah, September I think. [Records indicate that Derek was suspended on four occasions—two in September and two in October. No suspensions occurred since then.]

SP: I'm just amazed. When I see somebody who has made a change like you have, I always wonder how it was done. I want to know how you did those things.

DEREK: Man, I can't believe how I straightened up this year.

SP: It's remarkable, Derek. What made you decide to take control of the situation and take action to change like this?

DEREK: I don't know. I just wanted to. I want to do better. Not sit there at the Discipline Office all day.

SP: What have you learned about yourself in all this?

DEREK: What do you mean?

SP: Well, not everyone can do what you have done here, and I'm just wondering what these changes have taught you about yourself or how you will use what you've learned here in the future.

DEREK: Oh, I get it. I guess I learned that a lot of it is up to me. I mean, some teachers don't like kids, and they shouldn't be teachers. I'm sorry, but that's the way it is. Still, it doesn't do me any good to get in a bunch of trouble because I'm the only one who gets hurt from that. Teachers don't get in trouble. Other kids don't either. So I need to take care of myself, that's what I learned. If I screw up, it's my problem.

SP: Wow. That's a huge lesson to learn, Derek. What have you learned from this or about yourself?

DEREK: I learned that maybe I'm smarter than I thought, or that my teachers thought. I mean, I still have problems with math and stuff and I'm a really slow reader, but I can do some things better than I thought.

SP: Like what?

DEREK: Like answering questions in history class and writing simple stuff in English.

SP: That's important stuff. You made some big changes here, Derek. What does this say about you and the kind of person you are? [Helping Derek view progress as a consequence of his own efforts invites him to embrace a more heroic self-identity. His tone of voice is energetic and animated—quite a change from his presentation in the first meeting. Next, the practitioner and Derek explore "before-and-after distinctions" to encourage a more empowering story: one of competence, triumph, and tenacity.] What else is different at school since you started making these changes?

DEREK: My teachers are getting cooler.

SP: What do you mean?

DEREK: Well, they're just cooler. Like, they're cooler with me. Nicer and stuff.

SP: Why do you think they treat you nicer?

DEREK: I guess I'm treating them nicer (*laughs*).

SP: Oh. You mean the "new Derek" treats them nicer now than the "old Derek" did in the beginning of the year?

DEREK: Yeah.

SP: So the "new Derek" is nicer to teachers than the "old Derek."

DEREK: Yeah.

SP: And the teachers are nicer now to the new Derek than they used to be to the old Derek?

DEREK: Yeah.

SP: That makes sense. How do you treat them nicer these days?

DEREK: Just by not smartin' off, and trying to do better and stuff.

SP: So, you think you can actually kind of control what your teachers do by the way you act?

DEREK: What?

SP: Well, like when you do better, your teachers are cooler, right?

DEREK: Yeah.

SP: So, you kind of control their coolness by the way you act in class. When you're cool in class, it makes them cooler.

DEREK: Yeah.

SP: You never thought you could control teachers, did you?

DEREK: (*Laughs.*) No.

SP: How about other students? Are things any different with them?

DEREK: Not really. Well, maybe a little. They don't tease me and mess with me like they used to. This one kid, Thomas, he teases a lot, but he's cooler now.

SP: Wow. I was wondering if your dad is noticing anything different about the new Derek.

DEREK: Definitely. He's been in a great mood lately and I think he is just worrying about me less and the whole foster home placement thing.

Derek and the practitioner continued to explore other changes in his relationships with students and school staff. He even commented that the principal, whom he had viewed as out to get him, was nicer to him now. Next, the practitioner explores Derek's plans to maintain progress and prepare for possible setbacks.

SP: Do you plan to keep doing these things?

DEREK: Yeah.

SP: What can you do to make that happen?

DEREK: What?

SP: What can you do to keep things going good?

DEREK: Uh, come to class and keep getting good ratings and stuff. Not smart off, do my work.

SP: So you plan to keep doing the things you're doing now in class to keep getting good ratings and to be able to stay in school and with your dad.

DEREK: Yeah.

SP: You know, changes like this, big changes that are really hard to do, like the kind you've made in school, sometimes go a little back and forth. I mean, like you have real good days or even whole weeks that are pretty good. Then, you have a bad day when it's just like it used to be.

DEREK: Yeah, like last Friday right before we got out. I kind of lost it in math. Marcus said something about my dad, and I told him to screw off. I didn't scream it, I mean, like I used to, but Mr. Roth heard it and kind of got on me, made me apologize and stuff. I told him what happened and he made Marcus apologize to me. I said, "That's cool, he got in trouble, too." Which he should've, 'cause he started it.

SP: Yeah, so things like that will probably happen now and then. How did you do the rest of that class?

DEREK: What?

SP: I mean, after that happened with Marcus, were you cool, did you do okay in class after that happened?

DEREK: I just sat there and didn't look at Marcus no more.

SP: And you made it through the class without any more trouble?

DEREK: Yeah.

SP: That's great. I mean, that you made it through without losing it again. Three months ago you might have really lost it and got suspended or something.

DEREK: Yeah. I might have smacked him.

SP: So, when things sometimes go bad during a class, or somebody says something to you or about your dad or your family, you can stay cool and hold it together so you don't get sent to the office.

DEREK: Yeah.

Although students are relieved by improvements, they may fear that progress will not last. Addressing the possibility of setbacks helps students handle these normal bumps along the road of progress. Derek came up with several ideas: (1) looking away from people who tease him, (2) taking a deep breath when he's mad, and (3) saying "I'm sorry" when he messes up. The practitioner helped Derek translate these ideas into specific methods including deep breathing exercises and strategies for apologizing. Next, the practitioner invites Derek to join the Consultant Club, an advisory group of students who have changed their school behavior (Murphy, 1997).

SP: This is amazing, Derek. I don't know what to say. I'm totally impressed by what you've done. I wish we could make a movie of it so I could show it to other students.

DEREK: (*Laughs.*)

SP: I'm serious. In fact, I want to ask you if you would be willing to help me in my work with other students by being a member of my Consultant Club. This club is made up of students like yourself who have made important changes in their approach to school, and who are willing to share their wisdom and experience by giving me advice on how to help other students change things at school. If you agree to join this club, then I might call you sometime and ask you to help me out and give me ideas for helping other students make the kind of changes that you have made at school. Are you willing to do this?

DEREK: Sure.

SP: Thanks. I appreciate it, and I know other students will benefit from it.

The practitioner presented him with a certificate of membership in the Consultant Club, adding another chapter to the story of Derek's resourcefulness. This symbolized his recent accomplishments and served as a memento of the changes he made in his school behavior. Derek was also encouraged to celebrate and reward himself. He was planning to go fishing with his father on Sunday. The meeting concluded with Derek's rating of a 40 on the SRS.

Monitoring and empowering progress should include all major participants. The next conversation with Ms. Calhoun occurred several weeks after Derek's improvements in her class.

MS. CALHOUN: Things aren't perfect by any means, but a lot better.

SP: What do you attribute the changes to?

MS. CALHOUN: Well, maybe me making the first move and making a point of saying something positive to him early in the class period made a difference. He still has a lot of trouble with the work, but we don't argue as much and it's more like we're on the same side instead of enemies.

SP: I imagine it was pretty hard to make these changes, after all the hassles you had with him.

MS. CALHOUN: I was willing to do anything that would help calm the situation down so it wasn't like a tug of war to get him to cooperate. I'm just glad it's working.

SP: Me too. I have to tell you, your commitment to Derek through this whole situation is very impressive. With all you've dealt with, you've never given up. How have you managed to do that?

MS. CALHOUN: I really needed things to change and I was determined to find something that worked with him.

SP: Well, your determination has really helped Derek and he's lucky to have you as a teacher. Are you planning to continue with these changes you made in your approach to him?

MS. CALHOUN: Definitely. It's the schoolwork now that I need to look at.

Ms. Calhoun and the practitioner addressed Derek's difficulty with certain assignments. Ms. Calhoun's total ORS score was 26.6, an increase of 10.1 over her initial rating. The biggest jump occurred in the school area, which moved from a 2.3 in the first meeting to a 7.5 in this meeting. These scores reflected a substantial change in her perception of Derek. When asked to elaborate on the increase, she noted that Derek took school more seriously and completed more work. Ms. Calhoun's SRS score of 38 indicated a positive working alliance.

Although things weren't perfect, Mr. Roth and the other teachers reported that Derek was on the right track and making steady improvements. Mr. Roth no longer saw the need for further intelligence testing.

Mr. Brown was contacted by phone and asked again to rate how Derek was doing in school. He responded with a 7, adding that Derek seemed more interested in school and that the two of them were able to discuss school without arguing. When asked what he had done to make things better, Mr. Brown said that he was not getting on Derek as much and that he was spending more time with him. The practitioner validated Mr. Brown's strategies and reminded him that Derek's motivation to improve was largely tied to his desire to remain at home with him. Mr. Brown thanked the practitioner and expressed his appreciation for the work of everyone at school.

CONCLUSIONS

Although there were occasional infractions, they were less disruptive than Derek's previous problems. He completed the year without suspension, passed to 10th grade, and achieved his goal of staying with his father.

This chapter highlighted the three-E method of building solutions by utilizing exceptions to the problem. Derek expanded his success in social studies to other classes, paving the way for a more nuanced story of a kind, courageous, and determined student. Even in so-called chronic situations, practitioners can utilize "what works" and "what's right" by building on successes and other resources. Derek exemplifies our core premise that people are capable of heroic feats when given the opportunity to play key roles.

♦ ♦ ♦

Brief Intervention
Problem Busting

♦

Chapter 5 highlighted the solution-building interviewing format. Chapter 6 illustrates the problem-busting format. Recall that the two interviewing formats should be applied in a flexible manner based on the unique goals, preferences, and circumstances of clients. While most school problems are noticeable to teachers, the problem in this chapter was not detected despite its dramatic impact in the student's household.

REFERRAL AND BACKGROUND INFORMATION

Ms. Jordan phoned the practitioner in late January about her 10-year-old daughter. Maria, a fourth grader in a gifted program, achieved high grades in all subjects and was a cooperative and hardworking student. She lived with her parents and 7-year-old brother.

Ms. Jordan reported that Maria increasingly complained of headaches and stomachaches. She also insisted on staying up later at night and having her temperature taken in the morning. These out-of-character requests led to intense arguments between Maria and her parents. Making matters even worse, Mr. Jordan now had to verbally and physically coax Maria from the car into school when he dropped her off in the morning.

When Maria was examined by a pediatrician about her headaches and stomachaches, no physical difficulties were noted. The doctor recommended an antidepressant for Maria's "school phobia," but Mr. and Ms. Jordan decided to think about it and acquire more information. Meanwhile, Maria's grades remained high and no one from school reported any concerns.

ESTABLISHING CLIENT-DIRECTED PARTNERSHIPS

The practitioner met three times with Ms. Jordan and twice with Maria. As you read through this scenario, note how the Child Outcome Rating Scale (CORS) is used to establish a feedback culture and client-directed partnerships.

First Interview with Ms. Jordan

After initial greetings and small talk, Ms. Jordan completed the CORS: Me (3.6), Family (2.2), School (3.9), and Everything (5.1); Total = 14.8.

SCHOOL PRACTITIONER (SP): I can see by these scores that you're really concerned about your daughter right now. (*Explains what the numbers and clinical cutoff mean on the CORS.*)

MS. JORDAN: Like I told you on the phone, she's had almost completely straight A's since kindergarten and all of a sudden she has this school phobia thing. We don't know what's happening, or what to do with her. It's scary. I thought it would help if someone else talked with her. It's just really weird. We don't know what to do.

SP: Yeah, sounds pretty weird. Scary too. Like you've watched her pretty much cruise through school with no big problems, and now this.

MS. JORDAN: Yeah.

SP: You said "we" don't know what to do. Who else besides you?

MS. JORDAN: My husband and I. He's been trying to talk to her about this stuff. I've taken counseling courses too, and here we are. Makes you feel pretty dumb. We don't know what to do. So I finally said, "We've got to get some help on this." That's when I called you.

SP: I'm glad you called. I don't how it is with your kids, but with mine, this psychology and counseling stuff doesn't always help.

MS. JORDAN: (*Laughs.*) Yeah, I know.

SP: It's a lot easier for me to calmly listen to someone else's problem and think of ideas for them, than it is with my own problems or my kids' problems.

MS. JORDAN: Exactly. [This self-disclosure validates Ms. Jordan's experience and sets the tone for a client-directed partnership.]

First Interview with Maria

Ms. Jordan asked the practitioner to meet with Maria at home because Maria did not want other kids to think she was crazy. When the practitioner arrived, Maria was playing a computer game at the dining room table. Ms. Jordan introduced them and left the room. Maria played the game for 10 minutes while the practitioner sat in silence. She suddenly looked up and announced, "Okay, I'm ready."

SP: Okay. I'm glad you decided to go ahead with this chat. It takes courage to meet like this and to talk with someone you've never met. How did you muster up the courage to do this?

MARIA: I don't know. [Comments like this can help to establish a respectful tone and a perspective of clients as courageous and heroic.]

SP: I talked with your mother a couple days ago, but I'm interested in your take on things. I'd appreciate you taking a minute to fill out this form (*showing Maria the CORS*) to let me know how things are going for you. Will you help me by filling this out?

MARIA: (*Nods head "yes."*)

SP: Thank you. (*Maria completes the CORS: Me [8.2]; Family [6.1]; School [4.5]; and Everything [8]; Total = 26.8.*) [Maria's total score is 12 points higher than Ms. Jordan's, suggesting that she is far less distressed than her mother in all areas except School.] A score of about 33 or above says that things are going well. Your score, a

26.8, says that things are okay but not great, especially in school and your family. Is that right?

MARIA: Pretty much.

SP: I met with your mom and she filled out this form a couple days ago. It seems like she's pretty concerned about school and home too. She said things were pretty tense around here lately.

MARIA: (*Nods head, indicating "yes."*)

SP: Do you want things to change?

MARIA: (*Nods head, indicating "yes."*)

SP: Who do you think is more concerned about things—you, your mom, your dad, or James [Maria's younger brother]?

MARIA: James? He doesn't care. I'd say my mom or dad first, then me.

SP: Do you think your mom and dad have reason to be as concerned as they are?

MARIA: Not really. Well, some reason. But they make such a big deal of it.

SP: What could they do to be of more help to you right now?

MARIA: Just drop the school thing for a while. My dad keeps saying "You're not being reasonable; you're not being reasonable." I get tired of hearing it. It just makes it worse.

SP: Makes what worse?

MARIA: The school thing.

SP: What exactly is the school thing?

MARIA: You said you talked to my mother. Didn't she tell you?

SP: She told me that you ask to have your temperature taken. And that you ask them if you can stay up later at night and to not make you go to school.

MARIA: That's it.

SP: Anything you want to add?

MARIA: No, that's pretty well it.

SP: Your mom said things aren't going real well with Ms. Walker.

MARIA: That's one way of putting it.

SP: How would you put it?

MARIA: She's a witch, basically. She never smiles, she never talks to anybody except to yell at them. A real joy.

SP: Sounds like it. How long has this yelling and stuff been going on?

MARIA: All year.

SP: Wow. No wonder you're upset. How have you managed to hang in there and handle this without giving up?

MARIA: It's not easy. She is so mean.

SP: So does that stuff with Ms. Walker account for your mark on the School line being where it is (*picking up the CORS*)?

MARIA: Yeah.

This conversation supports a more heroic story of Maria and validates her perception of the problem and the teacher. Having connected the mark on the School line with her experience of the teacher, the practitioner and Maria are now on the same page about where things are and how progress will be noted.

THE THREE-STEP METHOD OF PROBLEM BUSTING

Recall that problem busting is useful when clients' attempted solutions are contributing to the very problem they are intended to resolve. The three steps of problem busting are (1) detailing the problem, (2) exploring solution attempts, and (3) interrupting solution attempts to allow for different responses to the problem.

Detailing the Problem and Exploring Solution Attempts with Ms. Jordan

This excerpt picks up in the first interview with Ms. Jordan.

MS. JORDAN: We're so frustrated. She's obviously troubled by something, and we should be able to help her, but we can't. We've tried everything. We feel like we're failing her. The weird thing is, nobody at school has even called, and she says she's doing fine in school.

SP: It's obvious that you and your husband have given this a lot of thought, and that you're very committed to helping your daughter any way you can. You haven't given up and you're willing to do what it takes to help Maria over this hurdle. That says a lot about you and your husband. I want to find out about some of those things you've tried, but first it would help me to get a better handle on the things she's doing, or not doing, that concerns you the most right now.

[Listening for heroic stories begins with Ms. Jordan's comment that "we've tried everything," which attests to the parents' commitment to helping their daughter. The story of failure is now nuanced with a story of dedication to Maria's welfare. Next, the practitioner obtains a clear description of the problem.]

MS. JORDAN: Okay. Every night, she tells us she doesn't want to go to bed, and begs us to stay up later. She'll say, "Please let me stay up. I promise I'll get up in the morning." At first we didn't let her, and she ended up going to sleep real late anyway. So we thought, "Hey, we've got nothing to lose, let's try letting her stay up an extra hour and see what happens." That didn't make any difference, either.

SP: So, is the biggest problem that she's staying up too late at night, or is it that she's giving you fits and arguing about it?

MS. JORDAN: Well, this might sound selfish, but the arguing and hassles are the biggest problem, because she eventually gets to bed and gets to sleep okay. But the arguing and carrying on upsets everything. Even James [Maria's 7-year-old brother] asks her to knock it off so he can sleep.

SP: Okay. I just want to make sure we're dealing with what's most important to you. So please excuse me for asking a bunch of questions. I just want to get a handle on exactly what's going on. So the arguing at bedtime (picking up the CORS), is that accounting for your mark here on the Family line?

MS. JORDAN: Yes, that's it.

SP: And if we make some inroads on that problem, we'd likely see your mark move to the right?

MS. JORDAN: Yes, definitely. [The practitioner connects Ms. Jordan's description of arguing to her mark on the Family scale. Next, the patterns surrounding the problem are explored.]

SP: Do you and your husband both deal with the bedtime thing, or one of you more than the other?

MS. JORDAN: Well, she and I have been locking horns a lot. We're more alike so I think we clash more. So my husband has been talking to her more lately. He usually tells her to go to bed about 9:00, and she starts asking to stay up later. We say "no," she argues and cries about it sometimes, and she eventually goes to bed.

SP: How does he tell her to go to bed? I mean, what does he usually say?

The conversation went on to detail concerns surrounding bedtime, temperature taking, and school drop-offs. This discussion, in combination with Ms. Jordan's CORS ratings, led to a two-part definition of the problem: (1) arguing about going to bed and taking her temperature (connected to the Family scale), and (2) refusing to enter school (connected to the School scale). Ms. Jordan reported that these behaviors had occurred every morning and evening on school days for the past 2 weeks.

When asked what she wanted from the consultation, Ms. Jordan replied, "We want our daughter back." The CORS was used to help Ms. Jordan describe the first signs that they were getting their daughter back. The practitioner pointed to her mark of 2.2 on the Family scale and asked, "What will be happening when this mark moves 1 or 2 centimeters higher?" Ms. Jordan replied that arguing and temperature taking would decrease.

Exploring solution attempts is the second step of problem busting. Next, Ms. Jordan's description of previous solution attempts clarifies her theory of change and steers the conversation toward what has and hasn't worked with Maria.

SP: What kind of theories do you have about what's going on with Maria?

MS. JORDAN: Well, the only thing we can think of is that she's afraid of failing, like a fear of failure thing. Because when we've asked her what's going on, she usually says, "Oh, nothing" or "I don't know" and asks us not to bug her about it. She doesn't even want to talk about it. We tell her the reason we ask is because we care, that we're trying to help her. I don't think she really believes that.

SP: Why do you think she doesn't believe that?

MS. JORDAN: Well, she usually gives you that blank stare, that look that means "when will this be over?"

SP: So what kinds of things do you and your husband usually say to her during these talks?

MS. JORDAN: Well, I tell her how I used to be scared to go to school sometimes. I was afraid of kids picking on me, and I told her that. I'm hoping that it will help her realize that other people have been afraid, too. So, maybe my anxiety is transferring to her, like she can sense my tension about it, and that makes it worse. So, that's why my husband has been taking over lately.

SP: How does your husband approach it?

MS. JORDAN: He's been talking to her about thinking straight, the rational thinking stuff, because she says her math teacher, Ms. Walker, is real mean and she seems real focused on this teacher. She says the teacher is real mean and yells at kids. The thing is, we asked her if Ms. Walker has ever yelled at her, and she said "no." She gets A's in math, she's always been good at school. I mean she's never had one discipline problem throughout school. So there's really no reason for her to be this afraid. She's getting A's and not getting in trouble.

SP: Does your husband talk to her about that?

MS. JORDAN: Yeah. He's a professional counselor, and he uses rational counseling a lot in his work. And so he points out that Ms. Walker has never really yelled at her. Plus, even if she does, how can that really hurt her? It's not something to be afraid of. As long as she studies and gets decent grades, a teacher can't really take anything away from her. We know about Ms. Walker. She's real strict with the kids, but she's not abusive or anything like that. That's just the way she teaches. So we're trying to get Maria to be more reasonable about the whole thing. Paul [Maria's father] tells her to think about the worst case scenario, like if she gets a B or C in this class. Big deal. We tell her, "We just want you to learn, and one B is not going to ruin your academic career." She catastrophizes the whole thing and gets herself all worked up. We want her to be able to face up to her problems and handle them, instead of trying to run away from them.

SP: So these talks don't seem to be getting through?

MS. JORDAN: No. I don't think so. She turns us off before we start. She says, "You don't understand." Then we say, "We know we don't understand. That's what we're trying to do. But you're not telling us anything." That's how it usually goes, and we both walk away disgusted.

Ms. Jordan went on to say that their talks with Maria ended up upsetting the whole household and making matters worse. The meeting ended in the following way.

SP: Before we stop, are there any other things you've tried, or even thought about trying, to turn this thing around?

MS. JORDAN: No. The stuff I told you, that's about it.

SP: Well, please think about that, and if you think of anything, give me a call, because we might be able to build on something you've already tried that works, or something you've thought of trying but haven't got around to yet. Okay?

MS. JORDAN: Okay. I'll let you know if I come up with anything. We'll do whatever it takes.

SP: I know you will. I can tell that you and your husband are very committed to seeing this through and doing whatever it takes to help Maria. She's lucky to have you as parents.

MS. JORDAN: Thank you.

SP: Before we end, I'd like your feedback about our meeting. This form (*handing Ms. Jordan the SRS*) is called the Session Rating Scale, or SRS for short. It's set up just like the other form that you filled out earlier (*referring to the ORS*), with four questions and a line to mark for each question. I need you to be totally honest on these forms because they tell me how I can be more helpful to you and how to make these meetings better. Okay?

MS. JORDAN: Okay. (*Completes the SRS: Relationship [9.3]; Goals and Topics [8.8]; Approach or Method [10]; and Overall [9.4]; Total = 37.5.*)

SP: When the marks are to the right like this, it tells me that you felt heard and respected, and that the overall approach was helpful. Your Goals and Topics mark is a little lower than the others. What other goals or issues could we have discussed to make the meeting even more useful to you?

MS. JORDAN: No, the meeting was really good. I feel relieved that we finally got help with this.

SP: That's good. Is there anything else I can do or we can discuss that would make our work even more useful to you? [The purpose of the SRS is to correct emerging alliance problems, no matter how small they may seem. Recall from Chapter 4 that the most effective practitioners elicit negative feedback from clients.]

MS. JORDAN: Well, we would appreciate any different ideas you have for us or Maria. We're open to any suggestions.

SP: I appreciate you telling me that. I'll think about what we've talked about today, and I will also be meeting with Maria this week. I'll let you know if I have any different ideas.

MS. JORDAN: Thank you.

Detailing the Problem and Exploring Solution Attempts with Maria

The first interview continues as Maria describes her concerns about her teacher and parents.

SP: So does this problem with Ms. Walker account for your mark on the school line being where it is (*picking up CORS and pointing to Maria's 4.5 mark on the School scale*)?

MARIA: Yeah. That's the problem. She's a witch, like I said. I'm too polite to use the other word.

SP: (*Smiles.*) That is polite, Maria. So, from your view, is it more of a problem that she's mean or that you're afraid of her?

MARIA: Both. If she wasn't so mean, I wouldn't be afraid.

SP: Have you told anybody that?

MARIA: I tell my parents all the time, but they want to talk to her and I don't want them to.

SP: Why don't you want them to talk with her?

MARIA: I just don't. I don't want anybody at school messing with me or thinking I'm crazy. But it's not like I want to be afraid, or like I'm trying to do this. I can't help it. But I'm not crazy.

SP: No, you're not crazy. I want to ask you about this mark (*pointing to her 6.1 mark on the Family scale*). You said your parents are on your case all the time about the school thing. Does that explain this mark on the family line?

MARIA: Yes.

SP: I know this is a weird question, but I'm wondering where this mark would be if your parents weren't on your case as much. You can just point with your finger.

MARIA: About here (*pointing to the "9" area of the Family scale*).

SP: That's interesting. So if we can find a way to get your parents off your case, things will be a lot better at home.

MARIA: Definitely.

SP: What exactly are they doing that bothers you most?

MARIA: They're always telling me that there's nothing to be afraid of, and telling me to ignore Ms. Walker and just do my work. They don't understand.

SP: Okay. So if we can figure out a way to get your parents off your case and to help you with this Ms. Walker thing, that will be a step forward, right?

MARIA: A big step. [Maria's experience of the problem is detailed and connected to her marks on the CORS. In the next excerpt, Maria is portrayed as a resourceful student who succeeds in the face of an intimidating teacher.]

SP: So when you say a witch, how bad is she? How mean would you say this teacher is, where 1 is like the nicest teacher there is, and 100 is the meanest?

MARIA: I can't go over 100? (*Laughs.*)

SP: (*Laughs.*) No, you can't go over 100.

MARIA: 95. No, 97.

SP: Wow. Mean city, huh?

MARIA: Totally.

SP: How do you manage to deal with this day in and day out? Your mom told me that you've kept your grades up in that class and in your other subjects. That's amazing to me. How do you do that with all this stuff going on?

MARIA: I try not to think about it.

SP: About what?

MARIA: About her.

SP: Does that help?

MARIA: No.

SP: What do you mean?

MARIA: It doesn't help. I try not to think about her, but I keep thinking about her.

SP: Is it like, the more you try not to think about her, the more you think about her?

MARIA: Yep.

SP: How do you know it's not working when you try not to not think about her?

MARIA: I just keep thinking about her when I try not to. I get all nervous in class. I even sweat.

SP: Holy cow. No wonder you don't want to go. [Maria's attempted solution had become part of the problem: The harder she tried not to think about the teacher, the worse it got.] So, what else have you tried?

MARIA: That's it.

SP: What do you want to see happen with this school thing?

MARIA: I just want it to be like it was. I mean, I never liked her in the first place, but this is crazy. I just want to go in her class and do the stuff without thinking about her. [Next, the practitioner brings the CORS into the conversation and invites Maria to "think small" by specifying the first few steps toward improving things at school.]

SP: Maria, you marked a 4.5 on the School scale. I'm curious what will be different when this mark moves up just a notch or two, like when it moves to a 4.6 or 4.7. How will you know that happened?

MARIA: That's not much of a change.

SP: No, it isn't. But I'm still wondering how you will know when the slightest change happens in that direction.

MARIA: My stomach won't hurt as much in school or in her class. I'll be able to concentrate better in there instead of freaking out. I won't be so worried about her, so I'll pay attention better.

SP: Is there anything else you would notice if things move up 1 or 2 centimeters on this scale?

MARIA: Well, she'll be nicer.

SP: How would you be able to tell she was just a little nicer?

MARIA: Maybe she'll smile more and say nicer things.

SP: Okay. Is there anything else you will notice when this mark gets a little higher?

MARIA: No, that's about it.

SP: Okay. How do you want to go about this? I mean, do you want someone to speak with Ms. Walker or do you want to try to work this out yourself and with your parents?

MARIA: Please don't say anything to Ms. Walker. That would make things worse, I promise you.

SP: So you would rather work this out yourself and with your parents?

MARIA: Yes.

Maria's perception of the problem and improvement were connected to her marks on the CORS. With the problem and solution attempts detailed, the stage is set for encouraging something different.

Interrupting Solution Attempts with Maria

The practitioner proposes an "experiment" to interrupt Maria's solution attempts and accommodate her mean teacher theory.

SP: I'm wondering if you could help me get a better handle on just how mean Ms. Walker is by keeping track of how many mean things she does during class.

MARIA: (*Smiles.*) What?

SP: It would be like an experiment to measure meanness. Like in science where they do experiments. They observe and keep track of things. You would have to observe real close so you don't miss anything. I could get a better idea of how mean she is if you would make a small mark in your notebook every time she does something mean. Remember, this is just observing and marking, not doing anything about it. Just observing and making the mean marks so we know what we're dealing with.

[Observing the problem without doing anything about it is different from the self-imposed pressure of prior solution attempts. This task combines two methods described in Chapter 3—"Observe the Problem" and "Invite What You Dread." These strategies are useful when clients are pressing too hard and trying to avoid unpleasant thoughts, feelings, or sensations. There is nothing magical about the task offered to Maria. The practitioner suggests it because it fits Maria's view of her predicament. Moreover, Maria is intrigued and readily accepts it.]

MARIA: Like during class?

SP: Yeah, during class, so you can mark it when it happens.

MARIA: (*Smiles.*) Okay, so you want me to count how many mean things she says during class?

SP: Not just the mean things she says. Things she does, too. She probably does things that are mean, too, doesn't she?

MARIA: Oh yeah.

SP: Okay. So, anything she says or does that's mean, mark it. You could just have a spot on top of the notebook page you're on that day, like this (*demonstrates*). Could you do that this week so we can get a good handle on this?

MARIA: I guess. It's kind of weird (*laughs*). I hope I have enough paper for it (*laughs*).

SP: (*Laughs.*) Yeah. Well, you can make real small marks, as long as you can see them well enough to count them. Another thing: It's important that you not laugh while you're doing this. You don't want to start laughing in class and call attention to what you're doing.

MARIA: (*Smiles.*) Nope. That wouldn't be cool.

SP: No, it wouldn't. [The practitioner's admonition shifts Maria's grim predicament to one in which she must now restrain herself from laughing.] You think you can do this?

MARIA: Yeah. I can do it. There's going to be a lot of marks, though, I'm telling you.

SP: So be it. Before we stop, I'd appreciate it if you'd fill out another short form like the one you did earlier. This one lets me know if we're on track here and if I'm being helpful. It also tells me what I need to do differently to be more helpful to you. Can you do that for me?

MARIA: Sure. (*Completes the CSRS: Listening [9.3]; How Important [9.1]; What We Did [7.2]; and Overall [7.1]; Total = 32.7.*)

SP: Thank you. So, you felt like I listened to you and we talked about important stuff. These marks (*pointing to the "What We Did" and "Overall" items on the CSRS*) are a little lower than the others. What else could I do, or do differently, to make our visit better for you?

MARIA: Well, it was fine, but I didn't think it was going to last this long and I've got homework and some other stuff to do. Plus, it's kind of hard talking about personal stuff.

SP: I really appreciate you letting me know about this, because I want these meetings to work for you. This meeting did run pretty long, didn't it? We've been here for over an hour, and that's a long time. I'll have to keep a better eye on that next time. I'll also be more careful about the personal stuff, too, because I don't want to get into any personal stuff that won't help us solve this teacher issue. What else could I do to make it better?

MARIA: That's it.

SP: Okay. How about we meet next week to check this out and see how things are going?

MARIA: Okay.

The "Observe the Problem" and "Invite What You Dread" task evolved from Maria's perception of the problem and her solution attempts—the problem cycle. Trying to avoid thinking about her teacher only made the problem worse. The task simply encouraged the interruption of that solution attempt in a way that accommodated her mean teacher theory.

Interrupting Solution Attempts with Parents

Mr. and Ms. Jordan were also stuck in a problem cycle: their solution attempts of lecturing and persuading perpetuated the very problem they were intended to resolve. The next excerpt is from the second meeting with Ms. Jordan, a day after the meeting with Maria.

SP: When we met a few days ago, you mentioned that the talks you and your husband had with Maria didn't seem to help.

MS. JORDAN: Right. It seems like we're talking to a brick wall. She just shuts down, especially lately.

SP: How willing are you to try something different?

MS. JORDAN: We'll do anything that will help her.

SP: Well, I'd like to get a better handle on how things go this week. I've asked Maria to try something in school. I'll let her tell you because she wanted to tell you herself instead of having me do it.

MS. JORDAN: (*Smiles.*) She told us about it last night.

SP: Okay. I'd like to ask a favor of you and your husband that's going to take some time and effort, but it might help us get a handle on how things go this week at night and in the mornings and on the way to school.

MS. JORDAN: Okay.

SP: I'd appreciate it if you and your husband could keep an eye on things while Maria is doing her experiment at school so we can tell when there's change, so we can recognize small improvements when they happen. Okay?

MS. JORDAN: Okay. Sure.

SP: This will give us a chance to see how Maria does with the school suggestion that she told you about. Plus, it gets you out of the tug-of-war business before your arms fall off. You know, the business of talking to her, her shutting down, and the whole thing upsetting the house like you said.

MS. JORDAN: (*Laughs.*) That sounds good. It's not working anyway.

SP: Exactly. Besides, backing off of talking to her a lot and making suggestions about school might actually give her some confidence. You know, it might convey your and your husband's confidence in her to improve things on her own. Who knows? That could send an important message of support to her.

MS. JORDAN: Yeah. I see what you mean. It's just hard to watch her suffering so much over this.

SP: It's got to be really tough, especially since she's never had any problems like this. It's going to be really hard not to jump in with ideas this week if you decide to do this.

MS. JORDAN: Oh, we'll definitely do it. It makes more sense than what we've been doing.

SP: Well, what you've been doing makes sense. It's just not working with Maria, so we'll take another road and see what happens.

MS. JORDAN: Sounds good.

SP: Can you help me out by filling out this form again (*handing Ms. Jordan the SRS*) just like we did at the end of the first meeting?

MS. JORDAN: Sure.

The practitioner encouraged the parents to discontinue their well-intended efforts to lecture, persuade, and counsel Maria. The observation task interrupted these solutions while honoring their desire to remain actively involved. Ms. Jordan's score of 39.2 on the SRS confirmed the fit of the task and her overall satisfaction with the meeting.

MONITORING AND EMPOWERING
INTERVENTION OUTCOMES

Outcomes were monitored and empowered during follow-up meetings with Maria and Ms. Jordan using the CORS.

The practitioner met with Maria for about 10 minutes 1 week after their first meeting. Maria opened the front door and greeted the practitioner by saying "Hi. It's not a problem any more."

SP: What's not a problem?

MARIA: The teacher. School. Everything's snappy.

SP: What do you mean?

MARIA: I'm not nervous about it.

SP: Wow, that's great. I can't wait to hear about this. Would you fill out this form for me again?

MARIA: Sure. (*Completes the CORS: Me [10; a 1.8-point increase from last week]; Family [9.5; a 3.4-point increase]; School [8.1; a 3.6-point increase]; Everything [10; a 2-point increase]; Total = 37.6 [a 10.8-point increase].*)

SP: Wow, this is a lot different!

MARIA: Like I said, it's not a problem anymore. You want to know how many marks I had?

SP: You bet I do!

MARIA: (*Opens her notebook and starts counting.*) Oh, let's see. A lot. 117. (*Laughs.*)

SP: 117! (*Laughs.*) Does that surprise you?

MARIA: Not really.

SP: 117 marks for 1 week. Wow. That's some major-league meanness. And you're not nervous about it?

MARIA: Nope. I mean, she is mean. 117 marks. Give me a break. I'm just not nervous about it anymore.

SP: Okay. So things are snappy, your ratings are higher, and your parents said things are a lot better this week. What's going on here? How would you explain these changes?

MARIA: I don't know. It just happened. I can't explain it.

SP: How did you manage to make this happen? What did you do?

MARIA: I have no idea. Really. That's all I can say. I told my friend I would come over her house after school today. You think we'll be done soon? [Maria's comment that "it's not a problem any more," combined with her CORS ratings, prompts the practitioner to empower these changes. Maria wants to wrap up the meeting as quickly as possible. Her preference for short meetings was also indicated on her previous CSRS.]

SP: Yeah. We can be done real soon. The only thing I have left to say is that you're on to something here. I don't know what it is, but you're onto something that worked really well for you.

MARIA: I'll say.

SP: Do you want to set another time to meet or just leave it open?

MARIA: Leave it open. I'll tell my parents if I want to meet again. Okay?

SP: That's great. Congratulations. (*Shakes Maria's hand.*)

MARIA: Thanks.

The conversation credited Maria for the changes and encouraged her to construct an explanation—her own heroic story. The practitioner handed Maria the CSRS and she promptly completed it. All ratings were high except the 8.3 on What We Did. Maria explained that it was lower because "Everything's okay now and there's really nothing to talk about."

Mr. and Ms. Jordan reported big improvements in the morning and bedtime routine. The practitioner opened the next meeting with Ms. Jordan by asking her to complete the CORS: Me (8.8; a 6.2-point increase from first meeting); Family (8.1; a 5.9-point increase); School (8.5; a 4.6-point increase); Everything (7.7; a 2.6-point increase); Total = 33.1; a 18.3-point increase).

SP: Wow, this is quite a change from where things were the first time we met. Your scores on this form went up in every area and your total score went up over 18 points. Amazing. Things have changed quite a bit, huh?

MS. JORDAN: Definitely. We have our daughter back again.

SP: What's it like having your daughter back again?

MS. JORDAN: (*Pauses and her eyes tear up.*) It's great. It's like this big weight has been lifted off our shoulders, and her shoulders.

SP: Wow. That must be nice.

MS. JORDAN: It is.

SP: I have to tell you, I'm really impressed that you've been able to stick to your plan of not lecturing Maria or giving her a lot of advice about the school thing.

MS. JORDAN: Well, it's working, so we're not going to change anything.

SP: Yeah, I know what you mean. Like they say, if it's not broke, don't fix it, right?

MS. JORDAN: (*Laughs.*) Right.

SP: I'm guessing there were times when it was really hard to resist jumping in and giving advice like you used to.

MS. JORDAN: Well, a few times, yeah. She'll say something that almost seems like she's baiting us, you know, trying to push our buttons. (*Laughs.*) Something about the teacher or school. But Paul and I just bite our tongue and that's usually the end of it. Or we'll say something like "Well, if that's the way you feel." But there haven't really been that many of those comments lately. It's like she's back to her old self.

SP: How did you ever come up with saying "If that's the way you feel"? I love that! I need to remember that one with my kids, and other parents I work with. [The practitioner credits the parent's resourcefulness in developing this simple and effective response.]

MS. JORDAN: I don't know which one of us said it first, but we've both used it a few times and it seems to work for both of us.

SP: That ingenious. It's such a simple and respectful way to respond to her in these situations.

MS. JORDAN: So far, so good.

SP: Yeah. I think it's great that you and Paul have stuck to the plan even in the face of these times when she tries to push your buttons. That's hard to do. Your data collection has also been great and I appreciate you keeping track of things and sending it to me each week. I know how hard it is just to make it through bedtimes and mornings, much less having to do these ratings. You've really helped Maria by doing all this. [The practitioner validates the active role of the parents.]

MS. JORDAN: Thank you. I hope so. I just hope things continue like this. Those 3 weeks were bizarre.

SP: Yeah. What are your plans in terms of how you're going to approach things in the future?

MS. JORDAN: Well, we're not going back to those arguments and mini-counseling sessions we tried to have with her. (*Laughs.*) I mean, I'm sure we'll have arguments, like anybody does, but not locking horns like we did where nothing gets done and everybody ends up upset.

SP: Does Paul pretty much feel the same way?

MS. JORDAN: Oh, yeah. He's just happy not to go through almost pulling her from the car in the mornings. Things are normal again.

SP: I know Paul has had to work a lot lately and we haven't had a chance to actually meet or talk on the phone, but please congratulate him for me on these changes.

MS. JORDAN: I will. Thank you.

SP: Congratulations. (*Shakes Ms. Jordan's hand.*)

MS. JORDAN: Thank you for all the help.

SP: You're welcome. It's been very inspiring working with you and Maria and your family on this. It's great how each of you pulled together and rallied to defeat this problem. It took a lot of courage and commitment to hang in there through all of this, but that's exactly what each of you did. It seems like there should be some kind of victory celebration to commemorate your success.

MS. JORDAN: (*Smiles.*) It's funny you mentioned that. Paul and I were just talking about that the other night. Maria loves this Italian restaurant in the city. The food is really good, and the waiters sing and do these silly skits. The kids really love it. It's been at least a year since we've been there, so we thought we'd celebrate by going there.

SP: That sounds great. In terms of where we go from here, how do you want to handle it?

MS. JORDAN: Well, I guess we don't really need to meet any more, but I'd like to be able to call you if we need to.

SP: Definitely. Call if you think I can help you. Also, I'd appreciate if you could keep track of things a little while longer and I could call you to see how things are going in a few weeks. What do you think about that?

MS. JORDAN: That's fine. These ratings are easy, plus, like you said, we'll be able to see if things keep going well.

SP: Speaking of ratings, would you mind filling out this Session Rating Scale?

MS. JORDAN: Not at all.

The practitioner empowered progress by giving parents credit for the improvements, encouraging reflection about their success, and validating their willingness to do something different. Ms. Jordan's score on the SRS was 38.5. She rated every area 10 except for the Overall category, which was an 8.5. She explained that she would appreciate parenting ideas to help her children to open up more. The practitioner promised to give this some thought and called a couple days later with strategies for promoting parent–child communication (Faber & Mazlish, 1990).

The practitioner called twice during the last couple months of the school year to follow up. Parent ratings on the CORS indicated successful maintenance of progress. On the final administration of the CORS, Ms. Jordan's total score was 36.9 and Maria's was 36.2—above the clinical cutoff for children receiving services.

CONCLUSIONS

The three guidelines of outcome-informed practice were prominent in this chapter. "The Client Knows Best" was illustrated by the practitioner's recruitment of Maria's and her parents' strengths and resources. For example, Mr. and Ms. Jordan's commitment was instrumental to the design of the intervention. "Reliance on the Alliance" was exemplified by the practitioner's validation of each person's struggle and perception of the problem. For example, the "Observe" and "Invite" tasks accommodated Maria's mean teacher theory. "If at First You Don't Succeed, Try Something Else" also played a large role. Maria and her parents were stuck in a vicious problem cycle—the harder they tried, the worse it got. When invited to try something different, they rose to the occasion with favorable results. Outcome feedback ensured that the process stayed on track. The one-dimensional stories of school phobia and ineffectual parenting were replaced by multidimensional stories of tenacity and creativity. The example of Maria also highlights how school practitioners can make a difference in a short period of time. Chapter 7 applies the three guidelines to an increasingly controversial topic in the treatment of children and school problems.

CHAPTER 7

◆ ◆ ◆

Medication, Children, and Schools
The Guidelines Still Apply

◆

with JACQUELINE SPARKS

This book advocates three guidelines for intervention with school problems. We have seen the importance of putting students', parents', and teachers' voices center stage in all decisions. We have also seen how doing this activates client resourcefulness and strengthens the all-important alliance. Finally, this book encourages an ongoing tailoring of intervention options based on client preferences and outcome feedback.

Then why an entire chapter on children and psychiatric drugs? We believe that *not* to talk about medications in a book about school-based intervention would be like ignoring the proverbial elephant in the living room. Prescriptions of psychotropic drugs for children and adolescents have skyrocketed in recent years. School practitioners face daily challenges to manage disruptive behavior and make recommendations about

Jacqueline Sparks, PhD, is an Assistant Professor of Family Therapy in the Department of Human Development and Family Studies at the University of Rhode Island.

a range of other difficulties. The lure of a quick fix is understandable, and medication seems a ready-made solution. To skip a discussion of medication would be to ignore a growing reality impacting children and those who work with them. The prescription elephant won't go away just because we don't talk about it.[1]

A medical response all too frequently is made outside the awareness and choice of those most affected. Diagnosis and medication prescription is often in the hands of "experts," while children's views are discounted. Parents and teachers, too, may be reluctant to offer an opinion or ask a question about other options or side effects. Medication may be the only choice offered when students are diagnosed with certain problems such as ADHD or bipolar disorder. The end result can be that children, parents, and school professionals are shut out of the loop—their questions, ideas, and solutions take a back seat.

This chapter explores how practitioners can expand the range of options even in circumstances that typically trigger prescriptions. By exposing the shaky empirical support for medication practices, Chapter 7 equips practitioners to privilege the client's voice in medication decisions, including both those who choose medication and those who don't. Chapter 7 critically examines the science that makes medication a foregone conclusion, enabling practitioners to integrate accurate information into practice, to view medication as one of many intervention options, and to allow client preferences to lead the way. In short, this chapter argues that the three guidelines still apply to medication decisions.

MEDICATION GENERATION

A 15-year-old girl enters school through the front door, then proceeds down the hallway and out the back, another no-show for the day. Jess finds it difficult to attend to classroom work, preferring to hang out with the pony she helps care for as a part-time job. At the school meeting, Jess's mother states that she found marks on her daughter's arms, apparently self-inflicted with her father's penknife. A referral to a psychiatrist is made, and Jess is prescribed an antidepressant.

---

[1]It is not our aim to discredit individual preferences for or experiences with medication, or to claim that medications may not be helpful for certain individuals at certain times in their lives. Instead, we hope to provide a counterpoint to common assertions, thereby making space for other options for student problems.

Jess is not alone. The past decade has seen an explosion of psychotropic medication prescriptions for the under-18 age group (Zito et al., 2003). For example, 11 million prescriptions for antidepressants were written for children and teens in 2002. That same year, 2.5 million children were prescribed antipsychotic drugs. By 2003, 5.3% of all children took some type of psychotropic medication. Like Jess, if a child sees a psychiatrist, the chance of leaving the office with a prescription rises as much as 60% (dosReis et al., 2005). If Jess lived in a foster home, she would be 16 times more likely to be medicated (Zito et al., 2003); if the diagnosis ended up bipolar disorder or ADHD, her chances of being on more than one medication at the same time would be as much as 87% (Duffy et al., 2005). In fact, the practice of prescribing two or more medications at the same time is now considered common practice (Bhatara, Feil, Hoagwood, Vitiello, & Zima, 2004; Zito & Safer, 2005).

The push to medicate young people is fueled by the belief that many child problems are due to a chemical imbalance that requires medical intervention. Web pages, doctors' office brochures, magazine articles, and T.V. ads describe depression, ADHD, mood swings, and the like as brain dysfunctions. Even when we know they are promotions from drug companies, pictures of neurotransmitters or talking serotonin cartoons are powerful, lasting images. This biological perspective is also backed up by impressive-sounding clinical studies. Social explanations or solutions are not accorded the same weight in the media as medical ones and are a distant second when it comes to research funding and marketing. As a result, claims are rarely questioned and the assumption that child and adolescent problems have a biological basis has become accepted fact.

Despite the press, biochemical imbalances and other so-called mind diseases remain the only territory in medicine where diagnoses are permitted without a single confirmatory test (Duncan et al., 2004). Antonuccio, Burns, Danton, and O'Donohue (2000) state, "There is no test available that would demonstrate that any patient has a biological depression as opposed to any other type, or even that such biological depressions exist" (Is There Evidence That Antidepressants Correct a Serotonin Deficiency?, ¶3). The National Institutes of Health concluded that there is no valid test for ADHD, and its causes remain largely speculative; further research would be needed to establish ADHD as a brain disorder (National Institutes of Health, 1998). Loren Mosher, psychiatrist and former Chief of the NIMH Center for the Study of Schizophrenia, concurred: "A critical review of the scientific available evidence reveals no clear indication of hereditary factors, no specific biochemical abnormalities, and no associated causal neurologic lesion(s)[for so-called mental illness]" (Mosher, n.d., ¶2).

Many point to neuroimaging research as proof positive of the biology of behavioral and emotional problems. A highly publicized study claimed to show that the brains of ADHD-diagnosed children were smaller than their non-ADHD counterparts (Castellanos et al., 2002). However, this study contained a significant flaw. The study's control group was 2 years older, heavier, and taller than the ADHD-diagnosed children, and body size is widely known to correlate with brain size (Leo & Cohen, 2003). Consequently, the smaller brain sizes of the ADHD-diagnosed children cannot be assumed to be the result of ADHD. There are numerous other studies that seek to connect abnormal brain structure to the ADHD diagnosis. However, as Leo and Cohen (2003) note with puzzlement, "after twenty-five years, and thirty-five studies, there is not a single straightforward experiment comparing typical unmedicated children with an ADHD diagnosis to typical controls" (p. 51). This most important comparison is missing from brain imaging studies that explore the biology of attention disorders.

Despite 50 years of efforts to find one, no reliable biological marker has ever emerged as the cause of any psychiatric "disease." Nevertheless, when problems arise for young people medication becomes the first-line safety net and other options take a back seat. In this process, students, parents, and teachers often play peripheral roles in deciding which path to take.

Consider how the "the client knows best" guideline is applied to Jess's situation in a way that puts other options on the table and draws in the voices of Jess and her mother (Ms. Taylor).

MS. TAYLOR: Jess, you can't keep doing this. I don't want you to hurt yourself. What's wrong? What do you want?

JESS: (*Shrugs shoulders and looks down.*)

SCHOOL PRACTITIONER (SP): Jess, we just want to make sure you're safe. What do you think will help?

JESS: I don't know.

(*Everyone just sits for a while. There is a genuine puzzlement and concern from everyone in the room—there does not seem to be a way out of the dilemma.*)

MOM: Jess, do you want to go see Dr. Stevens? He mentioned something about maybe medication could help.

JESS: No! I don't want to take any pills. I've got to do this myself.

MOM: Okay.

SP: Jess, do you want to talk with me and your mom, or maybe just one of us alone, about some of that stuff we talked about last week?

JESS: (*After a lengthy pause, thinking*) Yeah . . . I told my mom about Nick [Jess's boyfriend]. She knows we broke up.

SP: Is that what's bothering you the most now?

JESS: Yeah. That, and school sucks.

Jess, her mom, and the practitioner talk for a while about how Jess cuts herself to help with the emotional hurt. They also talk about Jess's boredom with her classes and her desire to work more to earn money and not "waste time" at school. They listen to Jess and value that she feels comfortable enough to let them into her world. All agree that the first order of business is for Jess to be safe. Since Jess is adamant about not wanting medication, they agree to set up a safety plan. The practitioner ensures that Jess is the primary architect of the plan, prompting her to identify strategies that she believes will work. Instead of cutting at night when she feels down, Jess plans to listen to music, get in her mom's bed, or call her friends. Jess writes the strategies down and signs an agreement to tell her mom or call the hotline number if she feels like it is not working. The plan would start immediately and Jess's mom would monitor it at home. The school practitioner would check on how the plan was going and evaluate Jess's progress on the ORS. Dealing with the academic problem would come later, once everyone felt that Jess was out of the woods regarding her urge to cut.

This scenario could have taken a hundred other directions. Applying "The Client Knows Best" and "Reliance on the Alliance," Jess was consulted for her opinions and ideas. It was a real struggle to work together as a team, but the patience paid off in a viable plan. There are many ways to reach desired ends. Not every child is Jess and not every parent will react the same way as Ms. Taylor. What will work can only be known one child and one family at a time. Based on "If at First You Don't Succeed, Try Something Different," the practitioner was prepared to do something else if the plan was not working and the ORS showed no results. When problems arise, medication need not be the first and only path of intervention. School practitioners can be confident that solutions can follow many paths when students, parents, and teachers guide the way.

CHILDHOOD PROBLEMS AND DIAGNOSIS

Michael, age 13, is home from residential treatment, reunited with his mother who is now attending regular Narcotics Anonymous meetings. When confronted about his "clowning" in math class, Michael makes a beeline for the door and is found hanging halfway up the flagpole like a frightened monkey. Within 1 week, Michael is diagnosed with early-onset bipolar disorder and prescribed anticonvulsant and antipsychotic medications.

"Early-onset bipolar disorder" has an ominous ring to it. At first glance, medication seems the most logical intervention for preventing a slide into more distress and coping with the disorder. Diagnosis is the sole gateway to medications, providing the official rationale for medical intervention. The belief that diagnosis can accurately identify discrete disorders is a key assumption underlying medication prescription. School practitioners may feel that they have little choice but to assume that a diagnosis explains what is wrong and provides a solution.

In spite of its widespread acceptance, the validity and reliability of psychiatric diagnosis is suspect. Validity refers to the ability of a diagnosis to distinguish one disorder from another or from normal human behavior. Kendell and Zablansky (2003), writing in the *American Journal of Psychiatry*, conclude that "at present there is little evidence that most contemporary psychiatric diagnoses are valid, because they are still defined by syndromes that have not been demonstrated to have natural boundaries" (p. 7). The authors make the point that psychiatric diagnoses fail the most basic definition of validity: They lack empirical standards to distinguish the hypothesized pathological states from normal human variation to the problems of life. The result is a set of murky, overinclusive criteria for an ever-growing list of disorders (Duncan et al., 2004).

Diagnostic validity is particularly suspect when it comes to children. According to the World Health Report, "Childhood and adolescence being developmental phases, it is difficult to draw clear boundaries between phenomena that are part of normal development and others that are abnormal" (World Health Organization, 2001, p. 50). The Surgeon General's Report similarly states:

> The science is challenging because of the ongoing process of development. The normally developing child hardly stays the same long enough to make stable measurements. Adult criteria for illness can be difficult to apply to children and adolescents, when the signs and symptoms of mental disorders are often also the characteristics of normal development. (U.S. Department of Health and Human Services, 1999, p. 7)

The notion of stable, fixed psychiatric syndromes does not fit the fluctuations of child development and adaptation to changing social environments.

Reliability has to do with whether or not most clinicians looking at the same array of symptoms will come up with the same diagnosis. If professionals independently agree regarding a diagnosis, it is considered reliable. Robert Spitzer, known as the architect of the *Diagnostic and Statistical Manual of Mental Disorders* (DSM), commented on the ability of the DSM to provide a sound basis for consistent agreement in clinical diagnosis: "To say that we've solved the reliability problem is just not true. . . . It's been improved. But if you're in a situation with a general clinician it's certainly not very good. There's still a real problem, and it's not clear how to solve the problem" (in Spiegel, 2005, p. 63). In other words, Michael might well be diagnosed with depression if he were seen by a different clinician, or he may not receive a diagnosis at all.

Consider bipolar disorder, a label increasingly used to explain childhood problems, including Michael's. Clinicians pick from a list of behaviors like expansive or irritable mood, extreme sadness or lack of interest in play, rapidly changing moods, defiance of authority, or strong and frequent cravings, often for carbohydrates and sweets. Many of these signs can be part and parcel of normal development and/or responses to situational stress. A bipolar diagnosis can last a lifetime; out-of-the ordinary child behaviors tend to be time-limited.

Unlike the alliance and the client's perception of progress, diagnosis does not predict outcomes. Since the dodo bird verdict confirms that no one approach is better than another for any given problem, diagnosis has little utility in identifying effective interventions. Finally, diagnosis leaves out key elements of the child's life, such as poverty or family problems. What may seem like abnormal behavior may be adaptive responses to life events such as living in a dangerous neighborhood, being harassed at school, or coping with a parent's absence. At the same time, what is normal in one culture may appear abnormal in another. Diagnosis assumes a universal standard of psychological health and does not make distinctions for cultural variation.

Returning to Michael, consider the practitioner's response to his diagnosis:

SP: Hey, Michael, how's it going?

MICHAEL: Not so good. The doctor says I have some kind of . . . I forget. Anyway, he gave me these pills to take. Mom says I should take them, but they make me feel weird!

SP: I saw what the doctor said in the report he sent me. It says that it seems like your moods kind of go up and down. Does that seem right to you?

MICHAEL: Yeah. Kind of. I never know if mom is going to, you know, go off again. It's hard to sit there in class when I keep thinking about that, so I just start joking around. Then Mr. Riley gets on my case, and I haven't even done anything so I say, "I'm outta here!"

SP: Wow. That makes a lot of sense. No wonder you wanted to do something to get that thought out of your mind for a while.

MICHAEL: So, you mean I'm not crazy?

After the practitioner validated Michael's experience, they talked about his home situation and the constant worry he felt as a result. It was important for Michael to make sense of his own experience and actions, and to understand these as reactions to stressful events. The practitioner refused to allow the diagnosis or his situation at home to get him off the hook. They brainstormed ways that Michael could deal with his stress without getting in trouble. The practitioner returned to the pills because Michael expressed discomfort with them. Referring to the ORS, the practitioner suggested that Michael monitor his response to the medication to determine whether it was working or making him feel worse. Based on that information, Michael could discuss with his mother and doctor the best path to take. In sum, the conversation was not about his diagnosis but about the things that meant the most to him and what he could do about them.

This example illustrates that (1) diagnosis cannot reflect the circumstances of the child's life and cannot specify a solution; (2) children can identify what is most important and collaborate on solutions regardless of the diagnosis ("The Client Knows Best"); (3) troubling behavior can be validated as making sense within the context of the child's life, because children do best when they do not see themselves as "damaged goods" but as coping with difficult circumstances and capable of change ("Reliance on the Alliance"); and (4) children know whether medication is useful and, with the help of adults, can be in the driver's seat in medication decisions ("If at First You Don't Succeed . . ."). The practitioner resisted diagnosis as the only story to be told about Michael, and instead trusted that a competing account of triumph over adversity could emerge.

EFFECTIVENESS OF CHILD PSYCHOTROPIC MEDICATIONS

Kyle, age 6, according to his parents, "flies into a rage at the drop of a hat." They note that Kyle's rages occur when playing with his 3-year-old sister, and they fear that he may hurt her. In a conference with the school practitioner, Kyle's mother (Ms. Mancini) shares her concern that he might have a mental illness. Children are routinely being medicated at younger and younger ages (Zito et al., 2000). When parents and teachers hear that even young children can be mentally ill and that problems result from undiagnosed disorders, it makes sense that they may adopt this point of view when other explanations are not readily available. The path to medical intervention often follows in the hopes that medication will improve the child's chance for success.

The decision to pursue psychotropic drugs is largely based on the belief that they work. People assume that Prozac and similar drugs are the intervention of choice for child and adolescent depression, and that stimulant medications are consistently effective for children labeled with ADHD. Similarly, common wisdom has it that when medication and counseling are combined, a booster effect occurs, producing better results than either alone. These beliefs are reinforced by websites and other media addressing child problems. Pediatricians and family doctors also endorse such assumptions based on published evidence from clinical trials.

The clinical trials most often cited for medication effectiveness include the two clinical trials that gained Prozac U.S. Food and Drug Administration (FDA) approval for childhood depression, conducted by Emslie et al. (1997, 2002) (hereafter called the Emslie studies); the Multimodal Treatment of ADHD (MTA) examining the efficacy of Ritalin versus behavioral and combined intervention (MTA Cooperative Group, 1999); and the Treatment for Adolescents with Depression Study (TADS) that compared Prozac, cognitive-behavioral therapy, and combination treatments (Treatment for Adolescents with Depression Study Team, 2004). Analysis of these studies reveals four flaws that challenge the effectiveness of medication: (1) inactive placebos/sugar pills, (2) clinician versus client-rated measures, (3) inadequate time frames, and (4) conflicts of interest (Duncan et al., 2004; Fisher & Greenberg, 1997; Sparks & Duncan, in press). The Emslie studies will illustrate the four flaws. Consider whether you would have recommended FDA approval of Prozac for child and adolescent depression.

Inactive Placebos/Sugar Pills

The gold standard for research is the randomized, double-blind, placebo-controlled trial. In this design, two groups are formed, presumably similar since they are randomly selected from the initial pool of applicants. One group gets the drug being tested; the other, a placebo. In this design, no one, neither study participants, researchers, nor assisting clinicians, should know who is in which group—that is, who is taking the real drug and who is getting the dummy pill. This helps eliminate the bias that comes when participants and researchers know who is in each group, and weeds out factors like hope and expectancy that could interfere with determining what is actually responsible for any differences found between groups. The validity of the trial depends upon the "blindness" of participants who rate the outcomes.

However, most studies do not use *active* placebos—pills that mimic the effects of real drugs. Rather, they use inert sugar pills as the placebo, which makes it possible for most participants and clinicians to tell who is getting the medication. Inert sugar pills, or inactive placebos, do not produce the standard side-effect profile of actual drugs—dry mouth, weight loss or gain, dizziness, headache, nausea, insomnia, and so on. Study participants are likely to be on the alert for these types of events, and many are familiar with these effects since they have been on medications before (Antonuccio, Danton, & McClanahan, 2003). Consequently, these subjects are likely to correctly identify which group they are in.

Researchers interview participants throughout the study to collect information about change and side effects. Ongoing interviews that listen for or actively ask about side effects can easily reveal active versus inactive pill takers, effectively unblinding the study and skewing results. In support of this theory, a meta-analysis found that, when studies used active placebos, little or no differences were found between the sugar pill and the drug (Moncrieff, Wessely, & Hardy, 2004). The Emslie studies used inactive, sugar pill placebos, drawing into question the integrity of the study's double blind. Evidence of the compromised double blind were apparent in the drug manufacturer's own records, where "it was not uncommon to see notations defining the patient's blinded treatment, or in some cases to find fluoxetine (Prozac) plasma concentration results" (U.S. Food and Drug Administration, 2001, p. 19).

Clinician-Rated versus Client-Rated Measures

The instruments chosen as primary measures in drug trials are clinician-rated. While client-rated measures are often used, they are secondary to those rated by clinicians. Client ratings of improvement frequently differ from clinicians', often in ways that run counter to findings of drug effectiveness. In both clinical trials that resulted in FDA approval of Prozac, no client-rated measures indicated superiority of the drug over placebo. However, both studies concluded that Prozac outperformed placebo. How valid can an assessment of improvement be if the client does not agree with it? In the first Emslie study, two out of four clinician-rated measures indicated a difference between the placebo and selective serotonin reuptake inhibitor (SSRI) groups. Two client-rated measures found no difference. Similarly, the primary measure of the second study failed to show a significant difference—all client-rated and two clinician-rated scales showed no difference. Out of seven, three clinician-rated measures showed significant differences between the experimental drug and placebo. If children *and* their parents do not detect improvement over placebo, how effective are the drugs?

Inadequate Time Frame

Standard time frames for clinical drug trials are 8–12 weeks. In contrast, most prescriptions for youth psychiatric medication assume that the drug will be taken for much longer. Assessing how well a drug does in an 8- to 12-week period cannot portray an accurate picture of the drug's performance in real life.

Differences between medication and placebo groups tend to dissolve by 16 weeks (Fisher & Greenberg, 1997). This means that even if a shorter time frame found the drug to be superior, the superiority is likely time-limited. Moreover, short-term trials do not reveal how many people will discontinue use after even modest time frames, or how many in a placebo group improve over time. Without longer term follow-ups, researchers cannot make accurate conclusions about effectiveness in everyday life. The Emslie studies were of 8 weeks' duration, calling into question their usefulness in real-world decision making.

Conflicts of Interest

A key component of evaluating any drug trial is learning who paid for it and what the authors' potential conflicts of interest are. The pharmaceutical industry's influence over scientific inquiry has, in some ways, become almost a cliché. In May 2000, the editor of the *New England Journal of Medicine* called attention to the problem of "ubiquitous and manifold . . . financial associations" of authors to the companies whose drugs were being studied (Angell, 2000, p. 1516). Why is it important to know who sponsors a study? One recent review (Heres et al., 2006) looked at published head-to-head comparisons of five popular anti-psychotic medications. In 9 out of 10 studies, the drug made by the company that sponsored the study came out on top.

Without an appreciation of the role industry influence plays in how the study is designed, carried out, and disseminated, it would be easy to accept bottom-line conclusions as fact. However, recent regulations now require authors to fully disclose their affiliations, allowing a more critical appraisal of any study's conclusions. The first Emslie study, published prior to disclosure requirements, did not identify author affiliations. However, the second and approval-clinching trial of Prozac for child and adolescent depression lists author affiliations on the first page. Here, readers learn that Emslie is a paid consultant for Eli Lilly, who funded the research and whose product was being investigated. The remaining authors are listed as employees of Eli Lilly and "may own stock in that company" (Emslie et al., 2002, p. 1205). Combining this information with the "unblinding" resulting from inactive placebos seriously calls into question whether the researchers, either employees or consultants of the company whose drug was under investigation, could, with so much at stake, reasonably remain objective.

Even government agencies and professional panels are subject to pharmaceutical influence. The National Institute of Mental Health (NIMH), a significant source of research funding for many pediatric drug trials, is a part of the National Institutes of Health, extensively investigated in recent years for ties to drug companies (Willman, 2003, 2005). The FDA is the purported government watchdog for undue industry influence. However, according to a recent review, financial conflicts of interest among FDA advisory members are common (Lurie, Almeida, Stine, Stine, & Wolfe , 2006). In contrast, but not supported by multibillion-dollar corporate entities, counseling for children and adolescents has a strong tradition of proven effectiveness (Diamond & Josephson, 2005; Kazdin, 2004; Michael & Crowley, 2002; Weisz, 2004). Nevertheless, the political and economic clout of drug companies has allowed medication to take its place at the head of the intervention table. Awareness of these facts, however, can help neutralize undue influence and allow a clearly formulated choice based on a weighing of the pros and cons and the preferences of each family.

The MTA and TADS

Just as the four flaws compromise the conclusions of the Emslie studies, they also challenge the MTA and TADS as a basis for youth psychotropic prescription. The Multimodal Treatment Study of Children with ADHD (MTA), the major trial supporting the superiority of ADHD medication, not only didn't use an active placebo, it lacked a pill-placebo control group altogether (MTA Cooperative Group, 1999). Consequently, it relied on evaluations made by teachers, parents, and clinicians who were not blinded to the intervention conditions. The only double-blind measurement (made by classroom raters) found no difference among any of the intervention groups. In fact, the subjects themselves (the 7–9-year-old children) rated themselves as no more improved when using medication than when using behavioral or community alternatives. Interestingly, peer ratings concurred with this assessment. The fact that neither blinded classroom observers nor the children themselves or their peers found that medication was better than behavioral interventions suggests that stimulant drugs offer no advantages over non-medication alternatives.

Regarding time frames, the MTA surpassed its predecessors because it evaluated outcomes at 14 months instead of the customary 8-12 weeks. The assessment occurred at the 14-month end point while subjects were actively medicated. However, behavioral intervention had long since stopped: End-point measures were taken 4–6 months after the last face-to-face contact. Thus, the end-point MTA comparison was between active medication and withdrawn behavioral intervention. This made the comparison hardly a head-to-head contest, making the slight superiority of medication (on 3 of 19 unblinded measures) a foregone conclusion. A 24-month follow-up of the MTA shows that the improvements of children on medication deteriorated (up to 50%), while the behavioral intervention group retained their gains (MTA Cooperative Group, 1999). At 24 months, the majority of parents in the behavioral group thought their children were doing well enough that they did not medicate them even after the study had ended (W. Pelham, personal communication, April 21, 2003).

Finally, consider the conflicts of interest. For those studies conducted before the disclosure requirement, a little sleuthing can help. An online database published by a nonprofit health advocacy group (Integrity in Science, *www.cspinet.org/integrity/*) reveals that lead MTA investigator Peter Jensen and at least five other MTA authors have significant ties to drug companies. Specifically, Jensen is listed as a consultant to Novartis, the makers of Ritalin, the drug under investigation in the MTA.

In the Treatment for Adolescents with Depression Study (TADS; 2004), out of four separate treatment conditions, blinding was attempted in only the Prozac and placebo groups. Placebos were inactive, calling into question the blind between these conditions. Second, the study's two primary measures were clinician-rated. Results from the two primary end-point scales mirrored earlier Prozac trials: one out of two clinician-rated measures indicated superiority for Prozac, whereas the adolescent and parent measures indicated no difference between placebo and Prozac. While other end-point comparisons in TADS favored the combined medication/cognitive-behavioral group, this cannot indicate superiority of combining an SSRI with cognitive-behavioral intervention since these were not blinded comparisons: Participants and investigators knew who was receiving the combination medication and cognitive-behavioral intervention and who wasn't. In addition, only the combined group included an additional pharmacotherapist who monitored dosage and "offered general encouragement about the effectiveness of pharmacotherapy" (Treatment for Adolescents with Depression Study Team, 2004, p. 809). Even the TADS investigators acknowledge that, because of inequities in conditions and lack of blinding, the " 'active ingredient' in improvement cannot be specified" (p. 818). Third, the TADS trial was 12 weeks in duration. Fourth, lead investigator, John March, has received funding from Eli Lilly (Prozac's manufacturer), and has extensive ties to the pharmaceutical industry (*www. integrityinscience.org*). Five of the 11 other researchers, Emslie included, have financially benefited from Eli Lilly funding (Lenzer, 2004).

When practitioners know what to look for (Does the study have a true double blind? Are outcome measures clinician- or client-rated? How long did the study last? Who funded the study and what are the authors' industry affiliations?) they realize that medication should not be privileged over other options and they can continue to be guided by client preferences and views of helpfulness. Equipped with knowledge of the four flaws, practitioners also have a powerful method for evaluating future studies without having to take the word of the latest headline or sound bite on the evening news.

Kyle and his mother, Ms. Mancini, are at a crossroads. It would not be hard to start down a path that saw his difficulty as the early signs of mental illness. Through this lens, a proactive approach might make sense, warding off a potential downward spiral before it becomes entrenched and intractable. However, knowing also that such an approach most likely means medication with its attendant risk and unproven efficacy, it also makes sense to explore other ways to understand and to resolve his and his family's dilemma. The school practitioner listens carefully to Ms. Mancini as she expresses her concern.

SP: I can certainly see that you have some concerns here. I really appreciate how you're trying to make sure that you know what's going on so that you can take action sooner rather than later. Usually, it's a lot easier to head things off at this age, rather than wait until the child is 8 or 9, when it is a lot harder.

MS. MANCINI: Exactly! That's what we [with Kyle's dad] thought too. That's why I wanted to speak to you. You know, since we moved here, and the new baby came, and starting the business and all, we hardly have time to sleep.

SP: Well, it says a lot about you that you could make the time to get in here today! How can we be helpful here at school?

MS. MANCINI: I don't really know. But, what you said about doing something now rather than later, did you think we should have him see a doctor, or have some kind of evaluation, maybe some medication or something?

SP: Well, that is certainly something that could be done. But, we don't really know if that will be needed at this point. Most of the time, we can do things here at school, and also recommend things at home, that can move things in a better direction. Children Kyle's age typically respond well to behavior plans. We can observe what's working for him and what we can do to build in some rewards for when things are going well. It would be helpful if you could do the same—see what is working or what isn't at home. Would you note the times that Kyle is getting along with his sister and when things are going well? (*Ms. Mancini nods in agreement.*) If we can meet again next week, we might have some better ideas of what's going on and where to go with things. Does that make sense?

MS. MANCINI: Yes, it does. Problem is, his dad and I are so busy, and the baby takes up so much of my time, we hardly pay much attention to Kyle these days except to tell him to do things, like get ready for bed or to stop doing things. Come to think of it, we don't even have time to get him in bed like we used to, with his favorite game and story.

Kyle's mother and the practitioner continued for several more minutes. This conversation detailed concrete steps that could be implemented at school and home. A follow-up meeting was scheduled to review progress and develop a behavioral plan based on Ms. Mancini's and the teacher's observation of what was working. Diagnosis and medication, while not discounted, were not the primary discussion topics. Instead, other ways of viewing and addressing the problem emerged from applying the guidelines advocated in this book—privileging Ms. Mancini as the source of wisdom and solution, validating her experience, and partnering with her to explore options.

SAFETY OF CHILD PSYCHOTROPIC MEDICATIONS

Jess's mother was torn. On one hand, she feared for her daughter's life and would do whatever it took to protect her. On the other, she was leery of medications, particularly ones not approved for children. Michael was placed on an antipsychotic and an anticonvulsant. All he knew was that he didn't feel right. His teacher noted that Michael no longer disrupted class, but instead put his head on the desk a good portion of the day. Many popular drugs are viewed as safe for children. However, safety is often tied to a lesser-of-two-evils argument. Many are willing to accept certain risks when the possible alternative is a child's school failure, drug abuse, crime, or suicide.

Most psychiatric medications for children are prescribed "off label." This means that the majority of frequently prescribed drugs do not have the requisite two clinical trials that show they are safe and effective. Included in off-label medications are the new antipsychotics and all anticonvulsants. Additionally, no studies support the efficacy or safety of prescribing multiple medications. All antidepressants, with the exception of Prozac, are prescribed off label for child and adolescent depression. The window of approved drugs for children is very narrow—far narrower than what might justify the robust prescription rates. Even those medications that are approved have risks that are often minimized in the decision-making process.

A thoughtful weighing of risk versus benefit is at the heart of any medication decision. Much of the data that has been collected raises concern. A systematic evaluation of 82 medical charts of children and adolescents treated with SSRIs found that 22% experienced some type of psychiatric adverse event (PAE), typically a disturbance in mood (Wilens et al., 2003). Estimates of PAEs in child and adolescent studies is complicated by inconsistent methods of collecting side-effect data (Greenhill et al., 2003) and benign or misleading assessments of data actually reported. In the first Emslie study, 6% of participants taking Prozac dropped out due to manic reactions, compared with 2% in the placebo group. If extrapolated to the general population, for every 100,000 children on Prozac, as many as 6,000 might be expected to experience this serious adverse effect. In addition, according to FDA documents, at least two participants receiving Prozac in this study attempted suicide (U.S. Food and Drug Administration, 2001).

Furthermore, TADS recorded six suicide attempts by Prozac takers compared to one by non-Prozac takers, with more than double the incidence of harmful behavior. After a review of published and unpublished trials, the FDA issued a black box warning for all antidepressants for children, alerting consumers and providers to increased risk of suicidality and clinical worsening (U.S. Food and Drug Administration, 2004). The Medicines and Healthcare Products Regulatory Authority (MHRA) in the United Kingdom took it further, banning all antidepressants (except Prozac, which can only be used with children over 8 when talk therapies have failed). Growth suppression and adverse cardiac effects have been noted as well (U.S. Food and Drug Administration, 2001, 2003).

ADHD drugs also have troubling records when it comes to side effects. Sixty-four percent of the children in the MTA reported adverse drug reactions: 11% were rated as moderate and 3% as severe. In March 2006, an FDA safety advisory committee called for stronger warnings on ADHD drugs, citing reports of serious cardiac risks, psychosis or mania, and suicidality. A memo from the FDA review team additionally stated that they were struck by the fact that signs of psychosis and mania could occur in children who had never been at risk for these before, at standard ADHD medication doses (Dooren, 2006). Despite the advisory committee's black box recommendation, the FDA decided to forgo a black box for all ADHD drugs, and instead to highlight risks on the label and include an information guide for parents with each prescription.

Stimulant medications have been associated with increased emergency room (ER) visits. A recent study conducted by the U.S. Centers for Disease Control and Prevention found that thousands of children taking stimulants wind up in the ER with chest pain, stroke, high blood pressure, fast heart rate, and overdose (Johnson, 2006). While many had legitimate prescriptions, others likely took the drugs for recreational or performance reasons. Prescription drug abuse has become the new drug habit for youth, with nearly one in five teens reporting abuse of prescription medications (Partnership for a Drug Free America, 2006). Finally, a recent review of the effect of ADHD drugs on children's growth found that the drugs moderately suppress both height and weight—the average suppression for a 10-year-old boy was three-quarters of an inch in height and 2 pounds in weight (MTA Cooperative Group, 1999).

Children like Michael are taking antipsychotic medications in record numbers (Duffy et al., 2005; Staller, Wade, & Baker, 2005). Side effects for these drugs in adults are well known, including irreversible movement disorders, obesity, and the risk of diabetes. Given that one in five visits to a psychiatrist by a young person results in an antipsychotic prescription, a sixfold increase in recent years (Olfson, Blanco, Liu, Moreno, & Laje, 2006), it's hard not to be alarmed at what these risks might mean for children.

A RISK–BENEFIT DECISION

School practitioners don't have to step outside their range of expertise to assist with medication decisions: They can help students, parents, and teachers get the message that there are many paths to preferred ends. The empirical evidence supporting the benefit of child medication is far from substantial, while concerns regarding how safe these drugs are continue to surface. The recently adopted report of the American Psychological Association (APA) Working Group on Psychotropic Medications for Children and Adolescents (2006) states the following:

> It is the opinion of this working group that . . . the decision about which treatment to use first (i.e., which treatment is the most favorable to the child) should be guided by the balance between anticipated benefits and possible harms of treatment choices (including absence of treatment). By this we mean that the safest treatments with demonstrated efficacy should be considered first before considering other treatments with less favorable profiles. For most of the disorders reviewed herein, there are psychosocial treatments that are solidly grounded in empirical support as stand-alone treatments. Moreover, the preponderance of available evidence indicates that psychosocial treatments are safer than psychoactive medications. Thus, it is our recommendation that in most cases, psychosocial interventions be considered first. (p. 175)

The report further points out:

> It also should be acknowledged that there are cultural and individual differences about how to weigh safety and efficacy data, and consumers (i.e., families) might weigh them differently. Ultimately, it is the families' decision about which treatments to use and in which order. A clinician's role is to provide the family with the most up-to-date evidence, as it becomes available, regarding short- and long-term risks and benefits of the treatments. (p. 175)

Knowing this means that when students experience difficulties, discussions about solutions can be open, creative, and evolving, encompassing a range of views about change based on each person's concerns, circumstances, and preferences. While medication may be useful for some children, it does not have to dominate intervention strategies or monopolize talk about change.

The decision of whether or not to medicate a child is one of the most difficult any family can face. A medical path is always a choice, and its pros and cons can be explored with medical and nonmedical professionals. School practitioners can encourage parents, teachers, and students to seek information from a variety of sources, including physicians or other helpers. Regardless of the source of information, practitioners can ensure that children and significant adults are in the driver's seat.

The following are recommendations for engaging students, parents, and teachers as central partners in developing solutions—whether medical or nonmedical—that fit each child and each situation.

1. Gather input from multiple sources including the student, parents, teachers, school records, and community providers.
2. Develop multiple frameworks for understanding the problem based on the perspectives of students, parents, teachers, and significant others. Include developmental, familial, and environmental explanations.
3. Develop a concrete plan of action. If medication is part of the plan, make sure that all involved, including the student, are aware of potential risks, adverse events, the meaning of off-label prescription, and the lack of studies supporting combining medications. Suggest resources for obtaining additional information about risks and benefits, including physicians and unbiased sources. Include discussion of a time frame for discontinuation of medication.
4. Work with students, parents, teachers, and others to implement the plan and modify it based on systematic feedback on the ORS. If medication is part of the plan, invite the student and others to view positive change as resulting from their efforts; "Given that some students take meds and they don't work, how is it that you made them work for you?" These kinds of questions encourage people to take ownership for successful outcomes.

CONCLUSIONS

This chapter equipped practitioners with a critical perspective of medication as the intervention of choice, and applied the three guidelines to situations involving psychiatric drugs. It is not an overstatement that pharmaceutical money infiltrates much of the information available regarding medications. Antonuccio et al. (2003) conclude, "It is difficult to think of any arena involving information about medications that does not have significant industry financial or marketing influences" (p. 1030). Lack of critical awareness takes on even greater weight where children are concerned because children trust adults to make good decisions on their behalf. An awareness of the relationship between a profit-driven industry and science, and what that science actually reveals, enables practitioners to assist students, parents, and teachers in making intervention decisions by permitting a fuller picture from which to construct solutions that take full advantage of their creativity and resources. No matter what path is chosen, school practitioners can be guided by an unswerving faith that even the most daunting difficulties can be resolved when clients lead the way.

CHAPTER 8

♦ ♦ ♦

Frequently Asked Questions

♦

This chapter tackles eight questions that often arise in our teaching, supervision, and training on brief intervention. Chapter 8 highlights the main points of the book and perhaps addresses questions that you may have about applying these ideas where you work.

1. *You emphasize putting clients first, but who is the client in school referrals?*

> I try to give students more respect and input, but sometimes it's hard to do that *and* stay on the same page with teachers and parents.
>
> —GLORIA, SCHOOL PSYCHOLOGIST

"Who is the client?" is a complicated question with school referrals because multiple people are involved. Students are the ultimate clients and beneficiaries of intervention services. However, most referrals come from parents or teachers who often view things differently than the student. What do you do when the teacher wants to change the student's classroom behavior while the student would rather work on making friends? Or when the parent views a problem as urgent and the student does not?

There is nothing more futile than trying to convince students that they have a problem when they don't think they do, or that they should work toward a goal that is unimportant to them. Instead of trying to talk students into other people's goals, we ask students what they want to work on and start from there. After all, you can't rearrange the furniture until you're invited into the house. Sometimes it is possible to negotiate different goals with students, parents, and teachers in ways that respect each person's position while working toward similar outcomes. For example, if the teacher or parent wants the student to take school more seriously, but the student does not buy into that goal, we might ask the student if she is interested in getting her teachers or parents off her case about school. Though worded differently, both goals are aimed toward similar outcomes—turning in more homework, arriving to school on time, behaving better in class, and so forth. Accepting each person's position, and negotiating goals accordingly, enables practitioners to maintain alliances with all involved clients while encouraging them to work toward compatible outcomes.

With these points in mind, we believe that students' voices and goals have been sadly underutilized. As the undisputed primary clients of school intervention, students are in an ideal position to contribute to the goals, tasks, and evaluation of intervention services. The next question elaborates on the importance of privileging the voice and input of students throughout the intervention process.

2. How do you justify giving a voice to students who are too young or too disturbed to know what's best for them?

> We have the answers; we just need someone to help us bring them to the front of our head.
> —MOLLY, 10-YEAR-OLD CLIENT

Children, much like adults diagnosed with a severe mental illness, have had a profound absence of voice in the delivery of services under the justification that they do not know what is best for them. This injustice is compounded by the fact that the most students are mandated for services, and thus are subjected to the whims, well intended as they are, of the adults who decide on their behalf. Under these oppressive circumstances, it is incumbent on practitioners to ensure that space is given for the child's voice.

Proponents of seemingly simple strategies—asking children how they understand things as well as what they need and want, and responding accordingly—may be accused of being naïve, ill-informed, or unqualified. However, helping young people make sense of their experience in ways that generate hope and engagement is well grounded in empirical evidence. Recent meta-analyses of the child outcome literature indicate that no one approach is superior to another for resolving complaints in key child problem domains—depression, anxiety, conduct disorder, and ADHD. Additionally, research confirms the pivotal role the alliance plays in the outcome of child intervention. What this research is telling us is that the child—his or her inner, family, and community resources—and the relationship that we form with him or her are the most potent factors of change. Giving children a voice builds on these most influential components.

Perhaps transcending the research support, working with youth facing dire circumstances for the past 20-something years has given us a faith in honoring children's voices that runs very deep—a trust in students to overcome adversity despite overwhelming odds. It is in precisely those situations in which children seem most destitute, desperate, or at their lowest ebb that the most caution need be heeded regarding inclusion of their voice. By privileging their ideas, values, and feedback, we place young people in the forefront of their own change and recognize them as the heroes of their lives, even when compelled to act in their behalf.

3. Cultural considerations have become increasingly important in the helping professions. How does brief intervention address cultural issues?

> To exchange one orthodoxy for another is not necessarily an advance. The enemy is the gramophone mind, whether or not one agrees with the record that is being played at the moment.
> —GEORGE ORWELL

In discussing culturally responsive counseling for minority clients, Ridley (2005) cautions practitioners against stereotyping by reminding them that "each client is unique . . . and each has a different story to tell" (p. 85). Ridley stresses the importance of a collaborative alliance by noting that minority clients "often enter counseling feeling powerless" and "often gain a sense of empowerment and ownership of the counseling process when they participate in their own goal setting" (p. 107). Culturally competent practitioners enhance outcomes by not imposing their goals on clients, but rather tailoring the intervention process to the people being served (Boyd-Franklin, 2003; Sue & Sue, 2003). These are useful guidelines for all clients; we recommend approaching every client as a unique individual with a distinct cultural heritage and worldview. Structuring services "one client at a time" is part and parcel to culturally competent practice *and* brief intervention.

Brief intervention accepts clients' goals at face value, enlists their idiosyncratic strengths and resources, and adjusts services based on their feedback. "The Client Knows Best" guideline exemplifies our intention to learn from clients. This stands in contrast to squeezing clients into predetermined intervention molds or rigid ethnic templates. These practices not only are compatible with contemporary views of culturally responsive intervention, but are supported by empirical research on what works (Chapter 2). Putting clients first provides built-in safeguards for culturally sound intervention services.

4. Evidence-based practice (EBP) currently is considered the gold standard in the helping professions. How does EBP figure into brief intervention?

> I admire those who search for the truth. I avoid those who find it.
> —FRENCH MOTTO

EBP is another idea from the medical model that has been shoehorned into school-based practice. Our intent here is not to demonize EBP—any approach can be just the ticket for a particular client—but rather expose its limitations because it is often wielded as a mandate for competent and ethical practice. Such edicts are gross misrepresentations of the data and blatant misuses of the evidence.

What exactly is an evidenced-based intervention? It is just an approach that has established itself better than placebo or intervention as usual in only two independent clinical trials. Such demonstrations of efficacy are not really saying that much; intervention of nearly any kind has demonstrated its superiority over placebo for nearly 50 years! This research, for all its pomp and circumstance, tells us nothing that we already do not know: Intervention works.

To be sure, there is a seductive appeal to the idea of making interventions dummyproof, where the users—the client and the practitioner—are basically irrelevant and all one needs to do is diagnose the child and apply the evidence-based treatment. The assumption is that specific technical operations are largely responsible for client improvement, that active (unique) ingredients of a given approach produce different effects with different disorders. In effect, this assumption likens intervention to a pill, with discernable unique ingredients that can be shown to have more potency than other active ingredients of other drugs.

There are (at least) two empirical arguments that cast doubt upon this assumption. First is the dodo bird verdict, which as we have seen, colorfully summarizes the robust finding that specific intervention approaches do not show specific effects or superiority over other models. While a few studies have reported a favorable finding for one approach or another, the number of studies finding differences are no more than one would expect from chance.

The second argument shining a light on the empirical pitfalls of EBP emerges from estimates regarding the impact of specific technique on outcome, as discussed in Chapter 2. Recall that Wampold's (2001) meta-analysis assigns only 1% of the variance of change to specific technique. Moreover, other factors have far more "evidence" supporting them. Wampold (2001) portions 7% of the overall variance of outcome to the alliance, and from 6 to 9% to practitioner effects. As demonstrated throughout this book, the largest source of variance (87%), virtually ignored by EBP, is accounted for by client factors. The "pill" view of intervention that EBP promotes is perhaps the most empirically vacuous aspect because the approach or technique itself accounts for so little of outcome variance, while the client and the practitioner—and their relationship—account for so much.

Intervention is not an uninhabited landscape of technical procedures. It cannot be described without the client and practitioner, coadventurers in a journey across largely uncharted terrain. EBPs simply do not map enough of the intervention territory to make them worthwhile guides. Given the data, we believe that any attempts to mandate EPB are misguided and far outreach the findings, obscuring the importance of the client and alliance to successful outcome.

5. You paint a dismal picture of diagnosis. Is there any place for diagnosis in brief intervention?

> A word carries far—very far—deals destruction through time as the bullets go flying through space.
>   —JOSEPH CONRAD

Simply put, diagnosis has never lived up to its original billing. Although it continues to serve logistical functions such as meeting state requirements or facilitating third-party payments, none of this is related to client outcomes. Diagnosis of psychological and behavioral problems is highly unreliable and invalid, especially with children and adolescents. Diagnosis fails to reliably distinguish between the so-called pathological states themselves, or between these disorders and normal development variations or problems of living. Given these validity and reliability problems, it should come as no surprise that diagnosis has also fallen short on its promise to predict outcomes and select interventions.

Despite scientific evidence and practitioner concerns about the usefulness of diagnosis, old habits are hard to break, as evidenced by the growing number of disorders in the *Diagnostic and Statistical Manual of Mental Disorders* (DSM). Whereas the original DSM included 66 diagnoses (American Psychiatric Association, 1952), the newest version includes 397 disorders (DSM-IV-TR; American Psychiatric Association, 2000). That's an increase of 600%, or about seven new categories per year, over the past 50 years! Are we really becoming that disturbed, or has the profession's fascination with diagnosis spiraled out of control?

We view diagnosis as unnecessary and sometimes harmful to the change process. As a vestige of the medical model and biological psychiatry, diagnosis implies that the problem resides within the client. This is problematic in several ways. In addition to lacking empirical support as a predictive or prescriptive tool (see Chapter 7), diagnosis deemphasizes the impact of situational and environmental influences. Diagnosis blinds children and caregivers to commonsense interventions and actions based on their own ideas and resources—modifying classroom instruction, changing parenting practices, altering study habits, and so forth. Diagnosis can also reduce accountability and persistence in problem solving. We have seen parents, teachers, and students become discouraged and give up in the face of medical "disorders" that appear impervious to everyday solutions.

We are not denying the pain of serious problems or the importance of people's struggles. Some people do experience a sense of relief from being able to name the problem. We would never take that away from them. That being said, our experience has led us to view diagnosis as more of a hindrance than a help in promoting change.

6. *The Outcome Rating Scale (ORS) and Session Rating Scale (SRS) have been shown to improve outcomes and provide accountability. Why aren't these measures used in schools?*

> I think this is a really good idea, asking me what I think.
> —JAMES, 14-YEAR-OLD CLIENT

The biggest reason these measures are not used is simply because school practitioners are not aware of them. Although the ORS and SRS have been empirically validated and widely used in other settings, this is the only publication that addresses their systematic use in schools. As research continues and news spreads, we foresee the growing use of client-based measures by school practitioners. These measures have already caught the attention of state funding agencies and third-party payers who are calling for consumer-driven services.

The only way that client-based assessment will become part of everyday practice is if local school practitioners experience that client feedback improves outcomes. And the only way for this to happen is if school practitioners just do it.

7. *How can a practitioner or school district get started using client-based feedback to evaluate and improve services?*

> Just do it.
> —NIKE SLOGAN

If you are considering evaluating the effectiveness of your individual work or your school program, you are already on the right track. You have reflected about the importance of formalizing the client's voice in directing intervention and the value of documenting proof of the benefit of your services. You have accepted that the best of us are not effective with everyone. Consequently, you have decided to do something to help those clients who are not benefiting, knowing that becoming outcome informed increases effectiveness and allows the luxury of being useful to clients who would otherwise not be helped.

As the old saying goes, the first step of any journey is the hardest. You have to just do it. Use the measures in your next meeting with a student, teacher, or parent. Start collecting data now. If you are a sole practitioner in a school, use the measures, collect data, and enter your ORS and SRS scores in an Excel sheet or available software. Excel will perform all the calculations you need and is not hard to learn. Appendix C offers an easy method of looking at your data to determine the checkpoint conversation and last-chance discussion points (Chapter 4). Get others to join you from neighboring schools. You can also join the heroic agencies list (visit *www.talkingcure.com*), which provides support for practitioners all over the world who are implementing the measures and putting clients first in the delivery of services. On the same website, check out the Heroic Agency Network to see if a school system near you is implementing the measures and can provide assistance.

Explore the possibility of a pilot or demonstration project—the cost is minimal. If your school system has a research or accountability division, discuss the measures as a way to prove the effectiveness of school-based services, and suggest a comparison between those schools that merely collect data to those schools that use the feedback to alter services. Connect the collection of outcome data to an existing or proposed project in your school or district; sometimes it's easier to tag along than to start something new. Find a way. Just do it!

8. *What are the implications of brief intervention for training programs?*

> The dogmas of the quiet past are inadequate
> to the stormy present.
> —ABRAHAM LINCOLN

Consider how practitioners have traditionally been trained: In graduate school we are taught the content deemed necessary for competence, tested on that content, and ultimately retested on licensing exams. After graduation, the emphasis on the areas of content thought to promote competent practice persists as we are required to get continuing education to maintain state licensure.

Training programs also require students to be supervised in practicum settings: The field places great value on experience, which is usually specified as hours of client contact. All states require participation in supervised internships and practice. Competent practitioners, therefore, are expected to emerge from training programs teaching specific content areas combined with supervised experience over time. Unfortunately, these methods have not been shown to matter much in terms of effectiveness (Sapyta, Riemer, & Bickman, 2005). Not training, not supervision, not experience—they have no impact on outcome! Why? Practitioners are trained in intervention models, are supervised, and practice in the absence of information about the response to the delivered services, *especially* from the client's perspective. Making matters worse, practitioners are notoriously bad at determining their own effectiveness, predicting clients who are risk for negative outcome, and identifying a troubled alliance.

Given current training and licensing standards, it is theoretically possible for practitioners to graduate, obtain a license, and work their entire careers without ever helping a single person! Outcome-informed training programs would go a long way toward correcting this problem while offering protection to consumers. Training, licensure, and standards of care could involve ongoing and systematic evaluation of outcome—the primary concern of those seeking our services. Rather than evidence-based practice, practitioners can be trained to tailor their work to the individual client via practice-based evidence. Available evidence suggests that such feedback improves the practitioner's effectiveness over time: People do learn and change when given the opportunity.

Several training programs across the country are requiring students to track outcome with every client they serve in practicum and internship. Building a culture of feedback with students—eliciting client perspectives about outcome and alliance to best tailor services—positions students to succeed in an evolving consumer-driven and accountability-focused world. Students find outcome-informed work a huge relief of the burden to be experts, knowing they can rely on clients to provide direction and keep them on track. Emphasizing effectiveness rather than competence in graduate training involves students in a paradigm shift, one that not only improves outcome one client at a time but also assigns those we serve key roles in the delivery of services.

CONCLUSIONS

Like most practitioners, we have read books that sound great but fall short in the real world. Every idea and technique in this book has passed the most important test of all: practical application to real-world problems. Research continues to help us unravel and apply "what works." This book represents our attempt to translate research into practice in ways that are accessible to anyone who works with school problems.

We have had the privilege of learning from the greatest teachers of all—students, parents, and teachers. The first edition of this book ended with a "last call for the client" in which we urged readers to be mindful of the client's potent contribution to outcomes. Ten years later, we reissue this call with even more evidence that clients are the heroes of intervention. We will continue to learn from our clients and invite you to do the same by putting clients first ("The Client Knows Best"), obtaining their input and feedback ("Reliance on the Alliance"), and adjusting services accordingly ("If at First You Don't Succeed, Try Something Different").

APPENDIX A

♦ ♦ ♦

Index of Client Examples

♦

Although client examples may be discussed in several places throughout the book, this table lists the chapter and page where they appear first.

Client	Chapter/page	Summary
Kenny	1/p. 1	Third grader; referred for evaluation; witnessed father's death; abused by mother; practitioner validated the story of Kenny as resilient; interventions emerged from his resilience and resources.
Charles	2/p. 9	First grader; classroom problems involving another student (Dwayne); problem was resolved following a chance event in the neighborhood.
Molly	2/p. 13	10-year-old; nightmares, and diagnosis of separation-anxiety disorder; previously saw several therapists and was astonished when the practitioner asked for her ideas; developed her own solution to the sleeping problem.
Margaret	2/p. 18	Well-respected veteran teacher; embarrassed about losing her composure with a student (Robert); alliance was enhanced when practitioner listened and validated her struggle.

Client	Chapter/page	Summary
Sarah	2/p. 19	14-year-old; group-home resident; viewed as despondent and socially withdrawn; ate junk food and watched a lot of T.V.; longed to be Cincinnati Bengal cheerleader; encouraged to organize a cheerleading squad; became more active and outgoing.
Mildred	2/p. 21	Grandmother of 10-year-old (Jimmy) diagnosed with ADHD; invited to "think small" and describe the first step toward improvement; intervention targeted Jimmy finishing his morning cereal.
Jamie	2/p. 29	9-year-old; referred for fighting on the bus; diagnosed with "borderline ADHD" and started on stimulant medication; problem persisted; bus route was changed and Jamie was dropped off first, with positive results.
Sean	3/p. 35	9-year-old; diagnosed with ADHD; bed-wetting and classroom problems; validated heroic story of responsibility and competence; practitioner explored Sean's ideas for "defeating the pee monster."
Ellen	3/p. 47	15-year-old; previous abuse; displayed self-mutilating behavior of cutting; elicited exception to the cutting problem; encouraged to be the "master at the control panel" when it came to cutting.
Isabel & Jorge	3/p. 47	Parents concerned about "constant emotional outbursts" of 13-year-old daughter (Alina); asked what they wanted to see continue in Alina; noted several strengths and exceptions; agreed to do what worked in preventing and effectively handling outbursts.
Tony	3/p. 48	14-year-old; reported experiencing anxiety attacks "all the time"; asked what was right in his life; described his love of triathlon events and training during which he experienced "liberation" from the anxiety problem; entered more triathlons with favorable results.
Beth	3/p. 53	Special education teacher of 8-year-old student (Jermaine) who behaved aggressively and rarely finished work; practitioner validated Beth's commitment and frustration, and conducted solution-building interview; Beth expanded exceptions by involving Jermaine's aunt and previous teacher in the intervention.

Client	Chapter/page	Summary
Pat	3/p. 57	Concerned and vocal mother who believed her 9-year-old daughter (Ann) suffered from "genetic depression" despite school reports that Ann was fine; repeatedly attempted to cheer up and console Ann at the smallest sign of sadness; practitioner validated Pat's concerns and conducted problem-busting interview; Pat agreed to try something else by providing environmental supports to counteract genetic depression.
Mark	3/p. 59	16-year-old; told practitioner he was depressed; when asked specifically "how" depression was a problem, reported difficulty concentrating on homework and tests; obtaining small details produced a more specific and changeable problem than depression.
Jamal	3/p. 59	Twelfth grader; suffered from depression related to his father's drinking; asked for details on about how he "does" depression; resolved to stop bailing his father out and to stay clear of his parents' problems.
Erik	3/p. 61	Single parent of 17-year-old (Brent); frustrated by Brent's excessive pot smoking; discussed previous solution attempts; when asked what he had thought about but not yet tried, Erik implemented his idea of requiring clean periodic urine samples in exchange for driving privileges.
Jim	3/p. 64	Eleventh grader; complained of insomnia; tried many strategies to "make himself" fall asleep; the harder he tried, the worse it seemed to get; practitioner suggested that Jim simply observe the sleep problem for a week; began falling asleep naturally and quicker when he stopped trying so hard.
Sandra	3/p. 65	Tenth grader; complained of depression and excessive sleeping; believed she "should" be happy and regularly tried to convince herself of this; the more she tried, the more hopeless she felt; encouraged to "Invite What You Dread" by giving depression its due and allowing herself to feel what she felt and to reflect on her worries and challenges; felt more energetic and slept less.
Cheryl	3/p. 66	Ninth grade teacher who withstood incessant criticism from a student (Tim); repeatedly defended herself to no avail; decided to "agree and exaggerate" instead of defending herself and arguing with Tim.

Client	Chapter/ page	Summary
Matt	3/p. 67	15-year-old; difficulty urinating in school restrooms because of anxiety; self-talk and relaxation strategies did not help and Matt felt hopeless; became angry about the situation; practitioner encouraged a change in the "doing" of the problem by inviting Matt to accept and allow anger to occur as he stood at the urinal.
Hannah	4/p. 91	13-year-old; referred by mother for cuts on her arms and disturbing writings in her school journal; rated herself 35.2 on the ORS; discussion of ORS ratings revealed recent split with her boyfriend, which accounted for the cutting and note writing, according to Hannah.
Carrie	4/p. 97	Twelfth grader; senior class valedictorian and volleyball team captain; sudden onset of panic attacks; rated herself very low on the initial ORS (total score of 12); met with practitioner three more times with no appreciable gain in ORS scores; in response to low and unchanging ORS scores across four meetings, and realizing that no one is effective with all clients, practitioner initiated "last-chance discussion" and addressed referral-out options; Carrie switched to another practitioner and experienced steady improvements and gains in her ORS scores.
Derek	5/p. 100	Tenth grader in special education program for students with learning disabilities; referred for disruptive classroom behavior and minimal assignment completion; practitioner conducted solution-building interviews with Derek, his teachers, and his father; expanded Derek's relative success in Ms. Smith's social studies class to his other classes; used SRS and ORS with Derek and his teachers to obtain feedback on the alliance and outcomes; empowered progress by crediting Derek, his teachers, and his father for successful outcomes.

Client	Chapter/ page	Summary
Maria	6/p. 125	10-year-old; referred by parents for sudden somatic complaints and "school phobia" related to a math teacher she perceived as mean and scary; practitioner validated each person's concerns; problem-busting interviews indicated that their attempted solutions perpetuated the problem; interrupted solution attempts by encouraging Maria to observe and record her teacher's meanness during class (vs. trying not to think about it), and asked parents to observe and record Maria's behavior (vs. lecturing); used SRS and ORS to obtain ongoing feedback and adjust intervention accordingly; empowered positive changes by linking them to commitment and efforts of Maria and her parents.
Jess	7/p. 148	15-yr-old; referred to psychiatrist for cutting herself and prescribed an antidepressant; adamant about not wanting to take medication; school practitioner met with Jess and mother to discuss other options; developed safety plan designed to replace cutting with alternative responses to emotional pain.
Michael	7/p. 152	13-yr-old; returning to school from residential facility and recently reunited with mother; fled school building after classroom altercation; diagnosed with "early-onset bipolar disorder" and prescribed anticonvulsant and antipsychotic medication; practitioner and Michael discussed his stressful and unpredictable home situation as a factor in his mood swings; encouraged Michael to monitor his response to medication and discuss it with his mother and doctor.
Ms. Mancini	7/p. 155	Mother of 6-year-old (Kyle) who feared he had a mental illness based on his sudden rages; practitioner validated mother's concern and focused on behaviors of concern vs. diagnosis; discussed problem-solving options including behavioral intervention and medication; Ms. Mancini decided to start with a behavior plan, monitor its effectiveness, and go from there.

APPENDIX B

◆ ◆ ◆

Outcome and Session Rating Scales

◆

This appendix displays the outcome and session rating scales used in brief intervention as described in Chapter 4. These scales are for illustration purposes only. The actual scales, which include 10-centimeter lines for each item, are free for individual use and may be downloaded from *www.talkingcure.com.*

Outcome Rating Scale (ORS)

Name: _____ Age: ____ Session #: ____ Date: _____

Looking back over the last week, including today, help us understand how you have been feeling by rating how well you have been doing in the following areas of your life, where marks to the left represent low levels and marks to the right indicate high levels.

EXAMINATION COPY

Individually
(Personal well-being)

|—————————————————————————————————|

Interpersonally
(Family, close relationships)

|—————————————————————————————————|

Socially
(Work, School, Friendships)

|—————————————————————————————————|

Overall
(General well-being)

|—————————————————————————————————|

Reprinted with permission from the Institute for the Study of Therapeutic Change (*www.talkingcure.com*). Copyright 2000 by Scott D. Miller and Barry L. Duncan.

Child Outcome Rating Scale (CORS)

Name: _____ Age: ____ Session #: ____ Date: _____

How are you doing? How are things going in your life? Please make a mark on the scale to let us know. The closer the smiley face, the better things are. The closer the frowny face, things are not so good.

EXAMINATION COPY

Me
(How am I doing?)

☹ |————————————————————————| ☺

Family
(How are things in my family?)

☹ |————————————————————————| ☺

School
(How am I doing at school?)

☹ |————————————————————————| ☺

Everything
(How is everything going?)

☹ |————————————————————————| ☺

Young Child Outcome Rating Scale (YCORS)

Name: _____ Age: _____ Session #: _____ Date: _____

Choose one of the faces that show how things are going for you. Or, you can draw one below that is just right for you.

EXAMINATION COPY

Session Rating Scale (SRS V. 3.0)

Name: _____ Age: ____ Session #: ____ Date: _____

Please rate today's session by placing a mark on the line nearest to the description that best fits your experience.

EXAMINATION COPY

| I did not feel heard, understood, and respected. | Relationship ├─────────────────────┤ | I felt heard, understood, and respected. |

| We did not work on or talk about what I wanted to work on or talk about. | Goals and Topics ├─────────────────────┤ | We worked on and talked about what I wanted to work on and talk about. |

| The therapist's approach is not a good fit for me. | Approach or Method ├─────────────────────┤ | The therapist's approach is a good fit for me. |

| There was something missing in the session today. | Overall ├─────────────────────┤ | Overall, today's session was right for me. |

Child Session Rating Scale (CSRS)

Name: _____ Age: ____ Session #: ____ Date: _____

How was our time together today? Please put a mark on the lines below to let us know how you feel.

EXAMINATION COPY

Listening

Did not always listen to me. ☹ |————————————————| ☺ Listened to me.

How Important

What we did and talked about were not really that important to me. ☹ |————————————————| ☺ What we did and talked about were important to me.

What We Did

I did not like what we did today. ☹ |————————————————| ☺ I liked what we did today.

Overall

I wish we could do something different. ☹ |————————————————| ☺ I hope we do the same kind of things next time.

Young Child Session Rating Scale (YCSRS)

Name: _____ Age: ____ Session #: ____ Date: _____

Choose one of the faces that shows how it was for you to be here today. Or, you can draw one below that is just right for you.

EXAMINATION COPY

APPENDIX C

♦ ♦ ♦

Making the Numbers Count

♦

Recall from Chapter 4 that the major purpose of outcome management is to identify those clients who are not benefiting from services to enable a collaborative discussion about the best course of action. We suggested that two points of service are particularly important to stop and take stock of how things are going—the checkpoint conversation and last-chance discussion meetings. Appendix C offers an easy method of looking at your data to determine the checkpoint conversation and last-chance discussion meeting points.

Not all clients or practitioners are alike. Using the same broad guidelines to evaluate services at a local community mental health center and a typical school system would make little sense because the clients in the two settings likely differ in ways that affect the nature, duration, and outcome of intervention. To develop valid guidelines for such instances, school practitioners need to determine how change happens for clients *in their particular setting*.

Methods for estimating how change takes place in a particular setting run the gamut from simple, crude, and inexpensive to sophisticated, precise, and costly. Appendix C discusses one simple and one highly sophisticated method for determining how change happens for clients in a particular context.

CHANGE-BY-MEETING CURVE

A relatively simple method for tracking the occurrence of change is based on the pioneering work of psychologist Ken Howard. Briefly, Howard et al. (1996) found, "a lawful linear relationship between . . . the number of sessions and the . . . probability of improvement" (p. 1060). The outcome literature frequently refers to this finding as the *dose–effect* relationship. By creating a change-by-meeting curve (CBMC) that shows the relationship between the number of meetings (dose) and outcome (effect), practitioners can determine the probability of success for a specific client by a given meeting time during intervention.

The process begins with collecting outcome data on a representative sample of clients. Simply set a specific time period (e.g., 1 school year) during which to gather results from all clients. Generally speaking, the larger the number, the more accurate the data will be in representing the clients that a given school or practitioner typically serves.

The next step is separating successful from unsuccessful cases, noting in particular the meeting at which each client met or exceeded the change in outcome scores indicative of "reliable change." For the ORS/CORS a difference of 5 points or more is evidence that the change is reliable or significant (Duncan & Sparks, 2002). In other words, the measured changes are greater than chance variation in the instrument or normal maturation of the client (Hill & Lambert, 2004).

The final step is charting the results for the successful clients on a graph with the number of meetings increasing along the bottom (*x*-axis) and the percentage of successful clients along the side (*y*-axis). Figure C.1 gives a hypothetical example of a CBMC of data collected at a middle school.

The total number of clients was 74, involving one school practitioner. A simple comparison of the number of successful to unsuccessful clients revealed that approximately 57% (42) of the clients who began intervention with this practitioner experienced significant or reliable change. Visual inspection of the graph also shows that the majority of these successful clients began change by the second meeting, and the overwhelming majority achieved a reliable change by the third encounter. So for clients in this sample, the checkpoint conversation should likely occur in the second session and the last-chance discussion by the third meeting. All of the clients in this sample who achieved a reliable change had done so by the fourth meeting. The obvious advantage to

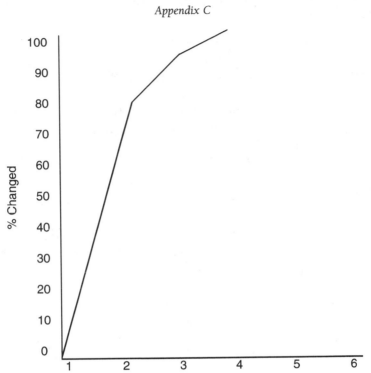

FIGURE C.1. Change by meeting curve data collected at a middle school.

this approach is that the client and practitioner can quickly determine whether intervention is progressing in a manner typical for successful cases *without* having to make any statistical calculations.

SIMPLE LINEAR REGRESSION

The word *simple* occurring in the same sentence as linear regression may strike some as oxymoronic. Truthfully, the average practitioner working in the schools can skip this section entirely without missing a great deal. In such instances, the CBMC will be sufficient for generating a dialogue with clients about the value of intervention. However, for those practitioners and administrators who require greater precision or need to compare the effectiveness of one program or school to another, the CBMC method will quickly prove seriously deficient.

A significant limitation of the CBMC is the curve's reliance on the reliable change index (RCI) to identify and separate successful and unsuccessful cases. As noted, a change in scores that exceeds the RCI can be considered greater than any variation in scores due to chance or the mere passage of time. The problem is that the RCI is an average, arrived at by aggregating clients of varying levels of severity. As a result, it is likely to underestimate the amount of change necessary to be considered reliable for some (i.e., those in the severe range) while overestimating the amount for others (i.e., those in the mild range).

In most school settings, it is not uncommon for a significant percentage of people seeking intervention to score in the mild range on outcome measures like the ORS or even above the clinical cutoff. A practitioner seeing many clients with relatively mild distress is likely to show a relatively small percentage of persons improving, according to the RCI. Indeed, a CBMC generated for such a practitioner might well show as many clients getting worse as improving, with a great many remaining unchanged. To compare that person's results to those of another whose clients scored mostly in the more-severe range would not be only unfair but also inaccurate.

The simplest method for dealing with this problem is to disaggregate the data and compare clients with similar levels of severity. For example, ORS scores at intake could be assigned to one of four differing levels of severity (i.e., quartiles) determined by the typical range at a specific school. The average change score could then be calculated for each of the four levels. The final step would be calculating the difference between the average and actual outcome for a given individual to determine if the outcome was better or worse than the average client in that severity range.

A more precise method is to use a simple linear regression model to predict the score at the end of intervention (or at any intermediate point) based on the score at intake. Although it is beyond our discussion here, briefly, it is possible to use the slope and an intercept to calculate a regression formula for all clients in a given sample. Software programs are available at *www.talkingcure.com* for computing expected trajectories and comparing practitioners and settings. Once completed, the formula can be used to calculate the expected outcome for any new client based on the intake score. This more precise method, analyzing the difference between the predicted change and the measured change over time and across clients, can be used to compare practitioners and schools. Such feedback about effectiveness improves outcome at both the individual and program level.

References

♦

American Psychiatric Association. (1952). *Diagnostic and statistical manual of mental disorders*. Washington, DC: Author.

American Psychiatric Association. (2000). *Diagnostic and statistical manual of mental disorders* (4th ed., text rev.). Washington, DC: Author.

American Psychological Association Working Group on Psychotropic Medications for Children and Adolescents. (2006). *Report of the working group on psychoactive medications for children and adolescents. Psychopharmacological, psychosocial, and combined interventions for childhood disorders: Evidence base, contextual factors, and future directions.* Washington, DC: American Psychological Association. Retrieved September 22, 2006, from *www.apa.org/pi/cyf/childmeds.pdf*.

Angell, M. (2000). Is academic medicine for sale? *The New England Journal of Medicine, 341*, 1516–1518.

Antonuccio, D., Burns, D., Danton, W., & O'Donohue, W. (2000). Rumble in Reno: The psychosocial perspective on depression. *Psychiatric Times, 17.* Retrieved June 16, 2006, from *www.psychiatrictimes.com/p000824.html*.

Antonuccio, D. O., Danton, W. G., & McClanahan, T. M. (2003). Psychology in the prescription era: Building a firewall between marketing and science. *American Psychologist, 58*, 1028–1043.

Asay, T. P., & Lambert, M. J. (1999). The empirical case for the common factors in therapy: Quantitative findings. In M. A. Hubble, B. L. Duncan, & S. D. Miller (Eds.), *The heart and soul of change: What works in therapy* (pp. 33–56). Washington, DC: American Psychological Association.

Berg, I. K., & Miller, S. D. (1992). *Working with the problem drinker: A solution-focused approach*. New York: Norton.

Bhatara, V., Feil, M., Hoagwood, K., Vitiello, B., & Zima, B. (2004). National trends in concomitant psychotropic medication with stimulants in pediatric visits: Practice versus knowledge. *Journal of Attention Disorders, 7*, 217–226.

Bohart, A., & Tallman, K. (1999). *What clients do to make therapy work.* Washington, DC: American Psychological Association.

Bordin, E. S. (1979). The generalizability of the psychoanalytic concept of the working alliance. *Psychotherapy, 16*, 252–260.

Boyd-Franklin, N. (2003). *Black families in therapy: Understanding the African American experience* (2nd ed.). New York: Guilford Press.

Brown, J., Dreis, S., & Nace, D. K. (1999). What really makes a difference in psychotherapy outcome? Why does managed care want to know? In M. A. Hubble, B. L. Duncan, & S. D. Miller (Eds.), *The heart and soul of change: What works in therapy* (pp. 389–406). Washington, DC: American Psychological Association.

Carroll, L. (1962). *Alice's adventures in wonderland.* Harmondsworth, Middlesex: Penguin. (Original work published 1865)

Castellanos, F. X., Lee, P. P., Sharp, W., Jeffries, N. O., Greenstein, D. K., & Clasen, L. S. (2002). Developmental trajectories of brain volume abnormalities in children and adolescents with attention deficit/hyperactivity disorder. *Journal of the American Medical Association, 288*, 1740–1748.

Dennis, M., Godley, S., Diamond, G., Tims, F., Babor, T., Donaldson, J., Liddle, H., Titus, J., Kaminer, Y., Webb, C., Hamilton, N., & Funk, R. (2004). The cannabis youth treatment (CYT) study: Main findings from two randomized trials. *Journal of Substance Abuse Treatment, 27*, 97–213.

de Shazer, S. (1985). *Keys to solution in brief therapy.* New York: Norton.

Diamond, G., & Josephson, A. (2005). Family-based treatment research: A 10-year update. *Journal of the American Academy of Child and Adolescent Psychiatry, 44*, 872–887.

Dooren, J. C. (2006, March 15). FDA urges stronger warnings on ADHD drugs. *Wall Street Journal*, p. D6.

dosReis, S., Zito, J. M., Safer, D. J., Gardner, J. F., Puccia, K. B., & Owens, P. L. (2005). Multiple psychotropic medication use for youths: A two-state comparison. *Journal of Child and Adolescent Psychopharmacology, 15*, 68–77.

Duffy, F. F., Narrow, W. E., Rae, D. S., West, J. C., Zarin, D. A., & Rubio-Stipec, M. (2005). Concomitant pharmacotherapy among youths treated in routine psychiatric practice. *Journal of Child and Adolescent Psychopharmacology, 15*, 12–25.

Duncan, B. L. (2002). The legacy of Saul Rosenzweig: The profundity of the dodo bird. *Journal of Psychotherapy Integration, 12*, 32–57.

Duncan, B. L., Hubble, M. A., & Miller, S. D. (1997). *Psychotherapy with impossible cases: The efficient treatment of therapy veterans.* New York: Norton.

Duncan, B. L., Miller, S. D., & Sparks, J. (2003a). *Child outcome rating scale.* Chicago: Authors.

Duncan, B. L., Miller, S. D., & Sparks, J. (2003b). *Child session rating scale.* Ft. Lauderdale, FL: Authors.

Duncan, B. L., Miller, S. D., Sparks, J. A., Claud, D. A., Reynolds, L. R., Brown, J., & Johnson, L. D. (2003). The session rating scale: Psychometric properties of a "working" alliance scale. *Journal of Brief Therapy, 3,* 3–12.

Duncan, B. L., Miller, S. D., & Sparks, J. (2004). *The heroic client: A radical way to improve effectiveness through client-directed, outcome-informed therapy.* San Francisco: Jossey-Bass.

Duncan, B. L., & Rock, J. (2005). *The lone changer: Solving relationship problems when your partner won't help.* Ft. Lauderdale, FL: WRWY Press.

Duncan, B. L., Solovey, A., & Rusk, G. (1992). *Changing the rules: A client-directed approach to therapy.* New York: Guilford Press.

Duncan, B. L., & Sparks, J. (2002). *Heroic clients, heroic agencies: Partners for change.* Ft. Lauderdale, FL: ISTC Press.

Duncan, B. L., Sparks, J. A., Miller, S. D., Bohanske, R., & Claud, D. A. (in press). Giving youth a voice: A preliminary study of the reliability and validity of a brief outcome measure for children and adolescents. *Journal of Brief Therapy.*

Emslie, G. J., Heiligenstein, J. H., Wagner, K. D., Hoog, S. L., Ernest, D. E., & Brown, E. (2002). Fluoxetine for acute treatment of depression in children and adolescents: A placebo-controlled, randomized clinical trial. *Journal of the American Academy of Child and Adolescent Psychiatry, 41,* 1205–1215.

Emslie, G. J., Rush, A. J., Weinberg, W. A., Kowatch, R. A., Hughes, C. W., & Carmody, T. (1997). A double-blind, randomized, placebo-controlled trial of fluoxetine in children and adolescents with depression. *Archives of General Psychiatry, 54,* 1031–1037.

Faber, A., & Mazlish, E. (1990). *Liberated parents, liberated children: Your guide to a happier family.* New York: Avon.

Fisch, R., Weakland, J. H., & Segal, L. (1982). *The tactics of change: Doing therapy briefly.* San Francisco: Jossey-Bass.

Fisher, S., & Greenberg, R. P. (1997). *From placebo to panacea: Putting psychiatric drugs to the test.* New York: Wiley.

Flexner, J. T. (1974). *Washington: The indispensable man.* New York: Little, Brown.

Frank, J. D., & Frank, J. B. (1991). *Persuasion and healing* (3rd ed.). Baltimore: Johns Hopkins University Press.

Goleman, D. (1991, December 24). In new research, optimism emerges as the key to successful life. *New York Times,* pp. B5–B6.

Greenhill, L. L., Vitiello, B., Riddle, M. A., Fisher, P., Shockey, E., & March, J. S. (2003). Review of safety assessment methods used in pediatric psychopharmacology. *Journal of the American Academy of Child and Adolescent Psychiatry, 42,* 627–633.

Haas, E., Hill, R. D., Lambert, M. J., & Morrell, B. (2002). Do early responders to psychotherapy maintain treatment gains? *Journal of Clinical Psychology, 58,* 1157–1172.

Hansen, N. B., & Lambert, M. J. (2003). An evaluation of the dose–response relationship in naturalistic treatment settings using survival analysis. *Mental Health Services Research, 5,* 1–12.

Heres, S., Davis, J., Maino, K., Jetzinger, E., Kissling, W., & Leucht, S. (2006). Why olanzapine beats risperidone, risperidone beats quetiapine, and quetiapine beats olanzapine: An exploratory analysis of head-to-head comparison studies of second-generation antipsychotics. *American Journal of Psychiatry, 163*, 185–194.

Hiatt, D., & Hargrave, G. E. (1995). The characteristics of highly effective therapists in managed behavioral providers networks. *Behavioral Healthcare Tomorrow, 4*, 19–22.

Hill, C. E., & Lambert, M. J. (2004). Methodological issues is studying psychotherapy processes and outcomes. In M. J. Lambert (Ed.), *Bergin and Garfield's handbook of psychotherapy and behavior change* (5th ed., pp. 84–135). New York: Wiley.

Hill, C. E., Nutt-Williams, E., Heaton, K., Thompson, B., & Rhodes, R. H. (1996). Therapist retrospective recall of impasses in long-term psychotherapy: A qualitative analysis. *Journal of Counseling Psychology, 43*, 207–217.

Horvath, A. O., & Greenberg, L. S. (1989). Development and validation of the Working Alliance Inventory. *Journal of Counseling Psychology, 36*, 223–233.

Howard, K. I., Kopta, M., Krause, M., & Orlinsky, D. (1986). The dose–effect relationship in psychotherapy. *American Psychologist, 41*, 149–164.

Howard, K. I., Moras, K., Brill, P. L., Martinovich, Z., & Lutz, W. (1996). Evaluation of psychotherapy: Efficacy, effectiveness, and patient progress. *American Psychologist, 51*, 1059–1064.

Hubble, M. A., Duncan, B. L., & Miller, S. D. (1999). Introduction. In M. A. Hubble, B. L. Duncan, & S. D. Miller (Eds.), *The heart and soul of change: What works in therapy* (pp. 1–32). Washington, DC: American Psychological Association Press.

Johnson, L. (1995). *Psychotherapy in the age of accountability.* New York: Norton.

Johnson, L. A. (2006, May 25). ADHD drugs linked to scores of ER visits. *Chicago Tribune*, p. 6.

Karver, M., Handelsman, J., Fields, S., & Bickman, L. (2005). A theoretical model of common process factors in youth and family therapy. *Mental Health Service Research, 7*, 35–51.

Kazdin, A. E. (2004). Psychotherapy for children and adolescents. In M. J. Lambert (Ed.), *Bergin and Garfield's handbook of psychotherapy and behavior change* (5th ed., pp. 543–589). New York: Wiley.

Kazdin, A. E., Marciano, P. L., & Whitley, M. K. (2005). The therapeutic alliance in cognitive-behavioral treatment of children referred for oppositional, aggressive, and antisocial behavior. *Journal of Consulting and Clinical Psychology, 73*, 726–730.

Kendell, R., & Zablansky, A. (2003). Distinguishing between the validity and utility of psychiatric diagnoses. *American Journal of Psychiatry, 160*, 4–12.

Lambert, M. J., Ogles, B., & Masters, K. (1992). Choosing outcome assessment devices: An organizational and conceptual scheme. *Journal of Counseling and Development, 70*, 527–539.

Lambert, M. J., Whipple, J. L., Hawkins, E. J., Vermeersch, D. A., Nielsen, S. L., & Smart, D. W. (2003). Is it time for clinicians to routinely track patient outcome? A meta-analysis. *Clinical Psychology, 10*, 288–301.

Lambert, M. J., Whipple, J., Smart, D., Vermeersch, D., Nielsen, S., & Hawkins, E. (2001). The effects of providing therapists with feedback on patient progress during psychotherapy: Are outcomes enhanced? *Psychotherapy Research, 11*, 49–68.

Lee, L. (2000). *Bad predictions*. Rochester, MI: Elsewhere Press.

Lenzer, J. (2004, September 4). Specialists' challenge claims that fluoxetine plus talk therapy works best for depressed adolescents. *British Medical Journal, 329*. Retrieved October 7, 2004, from *www.bmj.com*.

Leo, J., & Cohen, D. (2003). Broken brains or flawed studies? A critical review of ADHD neuroimaging research. *Journal of Mind and Behavior, 24*, 29–56.

Levitt, T. (1975, September–October). Marketing myopia. *Harvard Business Review, 53*, 19–31.

Luborsky, L., Singer, B., & Luborsky, L. (1975). Comparative studies of psychotherapies: Is it true that "everybody has won and all must have prizes?" *Archives of General Psychiatry, 32*, 995–1008.

Lurie, P., Almeida, C. M., Stine, N., Stine, A., & Wolfe, S. M. (2006). Financial conflict of interest disclosure and voting patterns at Food and Drug Administration Drug Advisory Committee meetings. *Journal of the American Medical Association, 295*, 1921–1928.

Martin, D. J., Garske, J. P., & Davis, M. K. (2000). Relation of the therapeutic alliance with outcome and other variables: A meta-analytic review. *Journal of Consulting and Clinical Psychology, 68*, 438–450.

Mayall, B. (2002). *The sociology of childhood*. Philadelphia: Open University Press.

Michael, K. D., & Crowley, S. L. (2002). How effective are treatments for child and adolescent depression?: A meta-analytic review. *Clinical Psychology Review, 22*, 247–269.

Miller, S. D., & Duncan, B. L. (2000). *The outcome rating scale*. Chicago: Authors.

Miller, S. D., Duncan, B. L., Brown, J., Sorrell, R., & Chalk, M. B. (2006). Using outcome to inform and improve treatment outcomes. *Journal of Brief Therapy, 5*, 26–36.

Miller, S. D., Duncan, B. L., Brown, J., Sparks, J., & Claud, D. (2003). The outcome rating scale: A preliminary study of the reliability, validity, and feasibility of a brief visual analog measure. *Journal of Brief Therapy, 2*, 91–100.

Miller, S. D., Duncan, B. L., & Hubble, M. A. (1997). *Escape from Babel: Toward a unifying language of psychotherapy*. New York: Norton.

Miller, S. D., Duncan, B. L., & Hubble, M. A. (2004). Beyond integration: The triumph of outcome over process in clinical practice. *Psychotherapy in Australia, 10*, 32–43.

Miller, S. D., Duncan, B. L., & Johnson, L. D. (2001). *The session rating scale 3.0*. Chicago: Authors.

Miller, S. D., Wampold, B. E., & Varhely, K. (in press). Direct comparisons of treatment modalities for pediatric disorders: A meta-analysis. *Psychotherapy Research*.

Moncrieff, J., Wessely, S., & Hardy, R. (2004). Active placebo versus antidepressants for depression. *The Cochrane Database of Systematic Review: The Cochrane Library, 2*. Oxford: Update Software.

Mosher, L. R. (n.d.). The biopsychiatric model of "mental illness." Retrieved June 10, 2006, from *www.moshersoteria.com/litrev.htm*.

MTA Cooperative Group (1999). A 14-month randomized clinical trial of treatment strategies for attention-deficit/hyperactivity disorder. *Archives of General Psychiatry, 56*, 1073–1086.

Murphy, J. J. (1997). *Solution-focused counseling in middle and high schools*. Alexandria, VA: American Counseling Association.

Murphy, J. J. (1999). Common factors of school-based change. In M. A. Hubble, S. D. Miller, & B. L. Duncan (Eds.), *The heart and soul of change: What works in therapy* (pp. 361–386). Washington, DC: American Psychological Association.

Murphy, J. J. (in press). Best practices in conducting brief counseling with students. In A. Thomas & J. Grimes (Eds.), *Best practices in school psychology* (6th ed.). Bethesda, MD: National Association of School Psychologists.

Murphy, J. J., & Duncan, B. L. (1997). *Brief intervention for school problems: Collaborating for practical solutions*. New York: Guilford Press.

National Institutes of Health. (1998). Diagnosis and treatment of attention deficit hyperactivity disorder (ADHD). *NIH Consensus Statement, 16*, 1–37.

Olfson, M., Blanco, C., Liu, L., Moreno, C., & Laje, G. (2006). National trends in outpatient treatment of children and adolescents with antipsychotic drugs. *Archives of General Psychiatry, 63*, 679–685.

Orlinsky, D. E., Rønnestad, M. H., & Willutzki, U. (2004). Fifty years of psychotherapy process-outcome research: Continuity and change. In M. J. Lambert (Ed.), *Bergin and Garfield's handbook of psychotherapy and behavior change* (5th ed., pp. 307–389). New York: Wiley.

Partnership for a Drug Free America. (2006). Generation Rx: National study confirms abuse of prescription and over-the-counter drugs. Retrieved July 11, 2006, from *www.drugfree.org/Portal/DrugIssue/Research/Teens_2005/ Generation_Rx_Study_Confirms_Abuse_of_Prescription#*.

Ridley, C. R. (2005). *Overcoming unintentional racism in counseling and therapy: A practitioner's guide to intentional intervention* (2nd ed.). Thousand Oaks, CA: Sage.

Rosenzweig, S. (1936). Some implicit common factors in diverse methods of psychotherapy. *American Journal of Orthopsychiatry, 6*, 412–415.

Sapyta, J., Reimer, M., & Bickman, L. (2005). Feedback to clinicians: Theory, research, and practice. *Journal of Clinical Psychology, 61*, 145–153.

Shadish, W. R., & Baldwin, S. A. (2002). Meta-analysis of MFT interventions. In D. H. Sprenkle (Ed.), *Effectiveness research in marriage and family therapy* (pp. 339–370). Alexandria, VA: American Association for Marriage and Family Therapy.

Shelef, K., Diamond, G. M., Diamond, G. S., & Liddle, H. (2005). Adolescent and parent alliance and treatment outcome in multidimensional family therapy (MDFT). *Journal of Consulting and Clinical Psychology, 73,* 689–698.

Shirk, S., & Karver, M. S. (2003). Prediction of treatment outcome from relationship variables in child and adolescent therapy: A meta-analytic review. *Journal of Consulting and Clinical Psychology, 7,* 452–464.

Simon, J. B., Murphy, J. J., & Smith, S. M. (2005). Understanding and fostering family resilience. *Family Journal: Counseling and Therapy for Couples and Families, 13,* 427–436.

Sparks, J. A., & Duncan, B. L. (in press). Do no harm: A critical risk/benefit analysis of child psychotropic medication. *Journal of Family Psychotherapy.*

Spiegel, A. (2005, January). The dictionary of disorder: How one man redefined psychiatric care. *New Yorker,* pp. 56–63.

Spielmans, G. I. (2006, August). *Specificity of cognitive-behavioral therapy for depressed and anxious youth: A meta-analysis.* Paper presented at the meeting of the American Psychological Association, New Orleans, LA.

Staller, J. A., Wade, M. J., & Baker, M. (2005). Current prescribing patterns in outpatient child and adolescent psychiatric practice in central New York. *Journal of Child and Adolescent Psychopharmacology, 15,* 57–61.

Sue, D. W., & Sue, D. (2003). *Counseling the culturally diverse: Theory and practice* (4th ed.). New York: Wiley.

Tallman, K., & Bohart, A. (1999). The client as a common factor: Clients as self-healers. In M. Hubble, B. L. Duncan, & S. D. Miller (Eds.), *The heart and soul of change: What works in therapy* (pp. 91–131). Washington, DC: American Psychological Association.

Treatment for Adolescents with Depression Study (TADS) Team. (2004). Fluoxetine, cognitive-behavioral therapy, and their combination for adolescents with depression. *Journal of the American Medical Association, 292,* 807–820.

U.S. Department of Health and Human Services. (1999). Children and mental health: Chapter 3. *Mental health: A report of the Surgeon General.* Rockville: MD. Available at *www.surgeongeneral.gov/library/mentalhealth/pdfs/c3/pdf.*

U.S. Food and Drug Administration. (2001, June 25). Medical review. Retrieved July 3, 2004, from *www.fda.gov/dcer/foi/nda/2003/18936SO64_Prozac %Pulvules_medr.pdf.*

U.S. Food and Drug Administration. (2003, January 3). FDA approves Prozac for pediatric use to treat depression and OCD. Retrieved January 25, 2003, from *www.fda.gov/bbs/topics/ANSWERS/2003/ANS01187.html.*

U.S. Food and Drug Administration. (2004, October 15). FDA launches a multi-pronged strategy to strengthen safeguards for children treated with antidepressant medications. Retrieved October 30, 2004, from *www.fda.gov/bbs/topics/news/2004/NEW01124.html.*

Walter, J. L., & Peller, J. E. (1992). *Becoming solution-focused in brief therapy.* New York: Brunner/Mazel.

Wampold, B. E. (2001). *The great psychotherapy debate: Models, methods, and findings*. Mahwah, NJ: Erlbaum.

Wampold, B. E., Mondin, G. W., Moody, M., Stich, F., Benson, K., & Ahn, H. (1997). A meta-analysis of outcome studies comparing bona fide psychotherapies: Empirically, "all must have prizes." *Psychological Bulletin, 122,* 203–215.

Watzlawick, P., Weakland, J., & Fisch, R. (1974). *Change: Principles of problem formation and problem resolution*. New York: Norton.

Weisz, J. R. (2004). *Psychotherapy for children and adolescents: Evidence-based treatments and case examples*. Cambridge, UK: Cambridge University Press.

Whipple, J. L., Lambert, M. J., Vermeersch, D. A., Smart, D. W., Nielsen, S. L., & Hawkins, E. J. (2003). Improving the effects of psychotherapy: The use of early identification of treatment and problem-solving strategies in routine practice. *Journal of Counseling Psychology, 50,* 59–68.

Wilens, T. E., Biederman, J., Kwon, A., Chase, R., Greenberg, L., & Mick, E. (2003). A systematic chart review of the nature of psychiatric adverse events in children and adolescents treated with serotonin reuptake inhibitors. *Journal of Child and Adolescent Psychopharmacology, 13,* 143–152.

Willman, D. (2003, December 7). Stealth merger: Drug companies and government medical research. *Los Angeles Times*, p. A1.

Willman, D. (2005, July 14). NIH inquiry shows widespread ethical lapses, lawmaker says. *Los Angeles Times*, p. A23.

World Health Organization. (2001). *World Health Report, 2001*. Retrieved July 22, 2006, from *www.who.int./whr/2001/en/whr01_en.pdf*.

Zito, J. M., & Safer, S. J. (2005). Recent child pharmacoepidemiological findings. *Journal of Child and Adolescent Psychopharmacology, 15,* 5–9.

Zito, J. M., Safer, S. J., dosReis, S., Gardner, J. F., Boles, M., & Lynch, F. (2000). Trends in the prescribing of psychotropic medications to preschoolers. *Journal of the American Medical Association, 283,* 1025–1030.

Zito, J. M., Safer, S. J., dosReis, S., Gardner, J. F., Magder, L., & Soeken, K. (2003). Psychotropic practice patterns for youth: A 10-year perspective. *Archives of Pediatric and Adolescent Medicine, 157,* 17–25.

Index